To My Dear Civilians, with Love

To My Dear Civilians, with Love

by **Rebecca Lord**
and **Brian Whitney**

BearManor Media
2016

To My Dear Civilians, with Love

© 2016 Rebecca Lord and Brian Whitney

All Rights Reserved.
Reproduction in whole or in part without the author's permission is strictly forbidden.

For information, address:

BearManor Media
P. O. Box 71426
Albany, GA 31708

bearmanormedia.com

Typesetting and layout by John Teehan

Published in the USA by BearManor Media

ISBN—1-59393-194-8
978-1-59393-194-0

Chapter 1

IT ALL STARTED WITH AN AD in a French newspaper. It was the kind of free newspaper that one finds in the mailbox mixed in with other commercial junk. The ad caught my eye even though it was in the middle of the apartment rentals and "cars for sale" ads. I noticed it because I found it so odd.

The ad said: "Looking for young women for erotic scene. For the casting call, please contact…" I was a bit shocked but also amused by the ad. Something drew me to it and for some reason I left it on my desk instead of trashing it, like I did with the other newspapers.

It was 1993 and I was 20 years old. I was living in Paris with my boyfriend, the man who later became my husband. He was working in the restaurant business and I was a make-up artist.

I was mainly working for photographers and directors of short films. I loved my job. If I can call it a "job" since most of my employers wouldn't pay me, because I was too inexperienced. So I guess one could say that I loved my no-money-job. It was exciting and I was around interesting people and for me at 20, while living in Paris, that was enough.

As a child, I grew up in the 15th arrondissement of Paris in a middle class environment. Shy and reserved, I grew up Catholic and received a very strict and religious education. As I grew older I had serious attitude issues at times. I believe most of this was due to growing up with religious bullshit and spending my youth in a very strict school. That's why, when I turned 17, I left my parents' home to live an independent life, no matter what the cost I had to pay. I would work for free, live modestly with very little money, I would work shitty jobs, and live in a tiny room. None of it mattered, I was free.

The last few years at home were hard for my parents and for myself as well. I had run away a few times. I had felt like I was suffocating.

I kept looking at the ad from time to time. It had gotten into my head. I would wonder to myself, "Is this for real? Who are those people?"

Of course, in my 20-year-old mind I imagined them as perverts. I had the typical image one has of a sleazy producer with a fat cigar, sweating and obese. The common image most of the people that never met anyone from the porn industry would have.

Was I right? Somehow I needed to know. In a way it was very "taboo" to me, but at the same time it sounded exciting, mysterious… I was curious and wanted to know badly what it was like! I felt like going there and not telling anyone.

Sometimes, life is about situations that come to you at a precise time. If I had not seen this ad when I did, my whole life would have been different.

Two years before then or two years after, I would never have gone there. But at that time of my life, I was all about confronting my fears, taking risks, trying new things, different things: I just needed it in order to feel alive. It was the perfect opportunity. I remember thinking: worse comes to worse, I'd get the hell out of there. What could happen really?

So I went!

The scene wasn't what I expected at first. I arrived at a little house in the suburbs of Paris, not too far from the city. It looked and felt like I was in the country.

This was it! There I was in front of the house. Suddenly, the weirdest thing happened: coming out of nowhere (or should I say: from the bushes next door, actually) a guy jumped in front of me.

The whole thing happened so fast I can't even remember his face; only that he seemed a couple of years older than me. He grabbed my arm and said that I shouldn't go alone in there and that these people could be dangerous. But HE was here for me and HE would protect me as long as we both said that we were together, as a couple. I was voiceless. I had no idea what was going on and honestly didn't have time to think of anything, since he was already knocking at the door.

A very pretty woman and her boyfriend welcomed us. They were both very friendly. I was still voiceless. I was even more confused because the supposed "bad guys" weren't what I was expecting at all. Anastasia and Patrice Cabanel were asking questions like: "did we both make the decision willingly?"—"did I know what I was doing and had I thought about it for a while before I came here?"—etc.

I then understood why the guy grabbed me. I just didn't know how to explain at the moment that the weirdo holding my hand and answering for me wasn't my boyfriend. I wished I had a sign that said "HELP!" Or at least a thought bubble over my head like in a cartoon!

My brain was boiling and felt like a pressure cooker. I think it showed because Anastasia understood very quickly what was going on. She threw him out, and I mean physically, and sent him along with some sweet insults!

The couple explained to me afterwards that it wasn't the first time some guy tried to use this trick to find his way into the adult industry. There were so many requests from men and so little spots to offer. Most of the adult productions are only seeking female performers. They need experienced performers in their movies and don't have time for newcomers.

A lot of wannabe actors use girls, or often their girlfriend, to get a chance to get in. They play the "couple" card. If the girl is real cute, and the guy is smart, lots of productions, to get the girl, will sometimes allow the man to be in the scene.

We talked for quite some time. I was stunned by their attitude and kindness towards me. This was not at all what I was expecting. They made me feel comfortable. After a while, as they requested, I took my clothes off so they could see my body. I did it the way you would take your clothes off in a doctor's office: as quickly as I could and clumsily.

It didn't take long for them to decide. They told me they wanted me for their next movie.

Wow! That simple? The meeting ended up with Patrice Cabanel telling me to think about it before I accepted. I had two weeks to give them an answer. I came back home totally confused.

Of course, "confused" also meant that I was surprised that I actually wanted to do the scene. This wasn't the initial plan! But my curiosity had taken hold of me. I had to see what came next.

It didn't take long for me to make up my mind. The only problem was Philippe, my boyfriend.

I had to tell him but I knew that there would be no way he'd accept it. I think he really thought I was crazy when I told him everything.

He had the same question for me that always comes up, even today, "Why?" I must say that I wasn't the stereotype. I had never watched a porn movie in my life.

So "why" would be a good question. I guess that every adult performer has a different answer, a different reason. Some of us even have more than one reason. Money, for instance, would be one of them. But as far as I'm concerned money was one of the many reasons why I stayed in this business so many years, building a career, not why I took the decision to "jump" in. Getting in and staying in are not motivated by the same reasons.

I think, at first, that my reason was truly provocation and rebellion. Rebellion against the education I received and everything that was imposed on me for so many years. Doing this movie was some kind of "exorcism" if you will. What's better than the use of sex to let go of these demons? Even though I wouldn't tell anybody and no one would know. It was just for my own satisfaction. This act itself was enough. It was MY life and I would be in control of it. No one else would make decisions for me.

Now go sell that to your boyfriend! That's another story! Philippe and I fought for days and had many arguments. Finally he understood that I wouldn't give up. The deal he came up with was that I wouldn't go by myself. The thing he really cared for above all was my safety. He would stay in the house in a different room in case something went wrong or if I needed him.

I had met Philippe in a pizza joint. He was the manager of the store and I was looking for one of those shitty extra jobs that I needed to pay my rent. To make it short: he hired me. We fell in love and had passionate sex everywhere in the pizza joint, after hours that is! He was working the night shift, I was still at the make-up school during the day, but we seized every opportunity we could get to have sex even if it meant being very sleepy during class. We had been together ever since.

Two weeks passed by quickly. I told Patrice Cabanel that I would do the movie even though I was way more nervous that I expected. I was pretty scared actually but I was excited at the same time. I wouldn't change my mind: now that I was there, I had to do it.

It was a real challenge for me and I liked it. Surprisingly, I can't remember details from the sex scene. What I most remember is the beginning of the scene when I had to take my clothes off in front of the camera: very slowly. That was kind of tough for me, the feeling of being watched by everyone.

I also remember the crew going back and forth to the other room. I found out afterwards that they were bringing glasses of water to my future husband who almost fainted (he could hear everything). I had to sign some paperwork in exchange for my paycheck. Obviously everything went well because everyone seemed satisfied and happy (except for Philippe).

I also recall the feeling of relief once it was over: I did it! I was so proud.

Over food and drinks, Anastasia and Patrice asked me if I thought about making a career being a porn actress. I laughed "Me??? Ahahahah!

No way!" However, they simply told me that if I ever changed my mind, they were here for me and would put me in contact with other productions. They were really nice the whole time.

I realized later on that I was lucky to have found them. Not every girl has such a good experience their first time. Like in every industry, there are good people and not so good people. Patrice and Anastasia were good people.

As I mentioned earlier, this would be my secret. No one will ever know. Of course they wouldn't: who is watching adult films? In my mind: no one, since I didn't! My conclusion was that if I didn't tell anyone, no one would ever find out. It would be impossible that anyone would ever know. Unless the pictures of my scene are published on a magazine's front page and that said magazine is displayed on every single newsstand in Paris!!! Which is exactly what happened.

I went straight to a lawyer and said, "They can't do this!!" Then after I read what was inside the magazine: "I never said those things! They can't publish that!" How naïve of me. Once you sign a model release, they can do whatever they please with your pictures, footage and interview.

I forgot to mention that there was a photographer taking pictures while I was doing my scene. I thought he was working for Patrice and Anastasia. He was actually taking pictures for both the production and a crappy porn magazine.

I remember thinking, "My life is over." In your circle of friends and family, this kind of news goes extremely fast. The phone started ringing. I couldn't pick it up. I was ashamed. Not ashamed of my actions but ashamed to be discovered that way. I felt like a thief when he is caught.

So I had a very stupid reaction. Instead of talking to them and explaining things, I withdrew into myself. Just like that, I assumed that everybody had a poor opinion of me. I found out later that some of them just needed to understand and be reassured. Not all of them though. There were a few people I never spoke to again.

As for my parents, a "good friend with good intentions" was kind enough to send them, by mail, the explicit magazine. Just to make sure they got the info correctly, of course.

It damaged them for a long time. Yes, it was my doing… but everything has to do with the way things are announced. Perception in life is everything.

I was enraged. Damage had been made and there was no coming

back. People judged me? My reputation was ruined? Fine. So be it. At that point, since everybody knew about it, I had nothing else to lose. I might as well keep up the pace. At least they will have something to judge and talk about. So, as the result of all that mess, I called Patrice and Anastasia and told them I wanted to work with other productions.

Chapter 2

THE WHOLE THING HAPPENED very quickly. Patrice recommended me to some friends and a few days later I was working for them. These were very similar productions: small budget, small crew. I found out later that this was known as pro-am: professional companies making amateur films.

I was surprised how comfortable I was during the hardcore scenes. I already knew the basics: I had to face the camera as much as I could without looking into it and listen to the director without looking or talking to him. It felt like I had done this for years.

The first movie was scary. I didn't know what to expect or do. Now that I knew what it was all about, I felt like nothing could go wrong. When you're scared, you are wide-awake. You absorb comments, info, visual signs, and chatter—your brain works very fast. In this particular situation it is a good thing. The truth is, in this business, you have to learn fast because no one will help.

Looking back at the whole thing one thing has been very clear to me. There is no doubt that before a sex scene, an interview, stripping on stage or simply signing autographs at a book store or at a convention… anything related to this job, it's like a second person inside me automatically comes out and takes control.

It is like I have a double personality. I feel that this other "person" was inside me all along and the adult industry gave her the opportunity to exist. Don't get me wrong. I am not saying I'm bipolar or something! Or trying to justify that some crazy person took over and I didn't know what I was doing.

I knew perfectly well what I was doing. I am just saying that most of us could have two different lives, like Jekyll and Hyde. Again, it's a matter of opportunity knocking at your door; once it comes you must seize it. Then comes the change of environment—in a specific environment people can react differently. The change of environment is quite intense when you become a porn performer!

Many of us live a certain way because of society and what is expected of us. I know I did. Now all of a sudden I was in a world where expectations were different, and I was just as comfortable in that world as I was in my more "normal" one.

After a couple of productions some people highly recommended that I get myself an agent so I could go to the next step: the world of professional porn. It would be easier for me than finding all of my own jobs. So I did.

I then found out that the rates for performing in a sex scene were not the same at all when you work for higher budget movies. The budgets for pro-am movies are fairly low in France. I also found out something quite interesting: I could "negotiate" what went on in my scenes.

When you perform sodomy for example, your rate goes up (a small detail that I would have appreciated knowing before, but…too late!). When you work with more than one person during a sex scene, your rate goes up! And so on… In fact, I learned that anything that was not a straight boy/girl regular scene has a different rate. If someone wanted me in a movie for a sodomy scene it would cost much more than if I were just to lie there on my back. Who knew? Not you I bet!

After meeting with the agent, he offered me a job stripping on a famous French national TV show. This was to be on public TV, not cable. If anyone didn't know about my sudden reconversion, after that show there was no doubt left. Then I was offered a trip to Roma, Italy, for two different jobs: a TV commercial for a perfume, for some guy called Rocco whatever, and a sex scene in a "big" movie for the same dude.

That guy just happened to be the biggest male porn star in Europe back then. He was perhaps the most notorious male porn star in the world during the '90s. Of course I am talking about Rocco Siffredi. Knowing nothing about porn, his name or notoriety didn't ring any bell whatsoever. As far as I knew I was just going to Italy to do a little movie and that was that.

Mister Whatever had his own menswear line in Italy and soon had his own perfume. After spending years being an adult performer, he decided to produce and direct movies. It was extremely rare (if not unique in Europe) in the early 90s, for an actor to get behind the camera. He was very famous, and still is, for his good looks, his performances and… his penis size! For good reason, mind you.

It was my first professional movie. What was impressive, compared to the pro-am movies I had done before, was the number of people on the set. There were between 15 and 20 people running around with tons of equipment, in a huge luxury house. I stayed and slept in the house for the entire shoot.

I was sharing a beautiful bedroom with another girl called Sandy. She was a gorgeous Italian woman who just turned 18 years old the day before.

I don't recall Sandy asking about who I was or what was I doing there, or any other conversation for that matter. All she talked about was Rocco: the man of her life. She had been in love with him since she was 15 years old.

I remember saying to her naively, "Oh? You guys are close?" Of course they were! She had been writing to him for 3 years and had seen all of his movies! Then she opened one of her bags. It was full of letters that they exchanged over the years, with hundreds of Rocco's pictures from magazines and such. Happily I didn't say, "Oh, that's him?" because I think she would have thought that I was insane.

She couldn't wait to meet him in person. She had waited so long for him so she could give herself to him as a virgin, and in front of a camera to immortalize that very moment. Tomorrow was going to be the best day of her life! She was so excited! She went on and on all night talking about him, not being able to sleep. Needless to say I didn't get any sleep either.

The beautiful Sandy had two scenes the next day. Sadly for her she started with a gang-bang, involving 10 guys, more or less. I bet the poor thing didn't plan it that way. I am not sure anybody explained to her the order of the scenes, or even what the scenes would be exactly. I don't think she had saved herself for Rocco just to be pounded on by a slew of men. Then, finally, she would do THE scene with her "boyfriend" and me.

The other big difference between a pro-am and a professional porn movie is the time spent on the set. Since the crew takes time to make things as perfect as possible (props, decor, lights, and sound), it can take hours. I would say it took between 3 to 7 hours for a scene, depending if there is dialogue before the sex or if there are some technical problems. A technical problem can be equipment breakdown, interruptions, cops, an unexpected "walk-in," and, of course, an actor that can't get "it" up. Understandably, the more performers there are, the longer the scene can last.

Sandy's first sex scene was a half-day scene. I took a peek once in a while, out of curiosity. I was stunned! Especially knowing she was a virgin. Imagine, 10 guys all over her! She didn't blink, didn't complain, didn't even ask for breaks and did an incredible job. How she pulled it off, I had no idea. At the time, I must confess it was a little scary to watch parts of that gang-bang and thought that I would never be able to do or handle something like it.

As for Mister Siffredi directing, he was always very nice, respectful, knew exactly what he was doing, and still kept enough distance from her to make things pretty clear: he was a director, not her lover. There was not a moment I saw him make her believe it was something else. It reassured me in some way—he wasn't a manipulator or anything of the sort.

After her scene was done, she took a few hours to relax. While she was taking a bath, I snuck in to talk to her. I wanted to know how she was doing. I think I was more shaken up than her just by watching.

She was crying. I freaked out. I was ready to take her away and call her parents. No…wait… She wasn't crying because she was traumatized, but because she was afraid her scene wasn't good enough for Rocco! He might stop loving her if it wasn't what he expected. Apparently Rocco forgot to mention to her how fantastic she was.

After what I witnessed earlier that day, how could I possibly show any shyness or embarrassment for my upcoming threesome sex scene? I mean, I just watched her get mauled by ten men and then I was going to be a coward?

Everything went fine. Not knowing who he was I wasn't expecting his penis to be quite so enormous. I certainly walked funny after the scene! Being part of that threesome didn't change a thing since Sandy was acting like I wasn't there anyway. It was actually less tiring, sharing Rocco between the two of us.

Rocco Siffredi and I have run into each other many times over the years, in Europe and in the US, during signings, conventions, interviews and such. I have the utmost respect for him. He is intelligent, classy, and successful and, did I mention, well endowed?

I never saw or heard again from Sandy. Apparently she never reached her goal of being Mrs. Siffredi.

I'M NOT GOING TO WRITE about every single movie I did. But some are really worth telling, not always in a good way though. The next movie I did after working for Rocco is a good example of this.

It was for a German company this time, but was shot in France, in the middle of nowhere. I went there for a day. I arrived very early in the morning. I was told I would be done by the beginning of the afternoon.

The shoot was in a three level house. It was decorated in a tacky way and dark, with only a few windows.

An assistant (or at least I thought he was, since he was the only person I ran into) told me to wait in a room, that they were running late. One hour went by and there was still no one around. Two hours passed, then three. I still didn't see anybody except for that same person passing through from time to time.

Suddenly he began telling me to get ready. He was jumping around like something bit him, and it was going be my scene next. Who I was working with, meeting with the director, a little conversation like human beings, a cup of coffee, apparently none of those were an option.

Another four hours passed, and soon five. I was getting really nervous. Even though I heard that sometimes you wait on a set for a very long time, I just didn't expect it to be this way. Left alone in a dark room and without any knowledge of what was going on, or would go on. It was not only rude—it was almost sadistic I thought.

At that point I had only done a few pro-am movies and one professional movie with Rocco. If it were now I would wait maybe an hour or so, then go to the set and ask the director what's going on. But that was then, and I was still a bit petrified.

I knew they were shooting upstairs because I could hear noises and footsteps. As the clock indicated six hours of boredom I was ready to interrupt everyone there. Just as I stood up, I heard someone screaming then rush down the stairs. She was crying and surely was mad as hell.

This is how I met Draghixa. She was "THE" French star at the time. All of a sudden she was in the room, standing naked in front of me. She was screaming while crying and I had a hard time understanding what she was saying. All I could hear seemed like insults. She calmed down after a few minutes and was getting dressed as fast as she could. "I'm getting the hell out of here!" She explained calmly that the director, Gabriel Pontello, peed on her while they were filming. She didn't see it coming since she was turning her back to the camera. She was shocked and humiliated. Of course they filmed everything, including her running away screaming, and them laughing at her. Unfortunately she had signed her paperwork before she did the scene (one thing I learned not ever to do that day), so there was no way to prevent the scene from being released. What a nightmare.

And then, she was gone. It was finally my turn. They were calling me upstairs.

I wasn't scared anymore. I was so angry with them! Don't get me wrong. I was worried that they would do the same to me, but I felt mostly anger.

The best way to protect yourself from people who intend to abuse you is to pretend you are tougher than them. Abusers are cowards. If I was willing to do the scene (the best decision would have been to simply leave; seems logical today but I don't know why it was not at the time) and I was, because I didn't want them to think I was scared, I had to put on my "war face." So I did. I played the "don't fuck with me" game! I looked at the director and talked to him like he was nothing.

Remembering that moment now makes me laugh. I never had to play that role again. It's just not me. I guess I can be bitchy sometimes; I had to be several times, but never like this.

The scene was quick. I refused to have my hands and feet tied up, like was initially planned. I learned an important lesson that day: you CAN refuse. You can say no. You can choose what you're willing to do and what you're not willing to do. A lot of girls in the adult industry, mainly in Europe, feel obligated to accept things even though they are not comfortable doing them, and in some cases, that's putting it mildly. This is wrong. The performers have power. A production cannot exist without them. The production will have no choice. They will run out of time, would have to reshoot the scene and hire someone else. And in this business, like in most, time is money.

Anyway, we faked a little S&M and went straight to the sex part. I was cold as ice with the actor but it didn't seem to interfere with his performance. Nothing happened to me. I will never know if my "war face" worked or if his bladder was just completely empty!

GABRIEL PONTELLO IS THE OPPOSITE of Rocco. He gives a very bad image of our industry.

Happily, I must say that, during my career, I rarely encountered sleazy people like Pontello.

Those experiences made me change my mind about working with an agent. I would rather be by myself, even if it meant less work. Trusting my agent after he sent me to Pontello, knowing fully what could happen (I learned later he was notorious for peeing on the girls), and not wanting to work for more creepy people, I decided to call a few people to find a good job and I hired another agent who was apparently more professional.

Right away it appeared that the new agent found my dream job. I went to a casting for a real estate agency that needed a girl, for pictures only: bathing suit photos to be specific, not even nude ones. Two weeks paid in the Easter Islands, for only three days work! Wooohooo! As soon as I found out, I went straight to the casting.

The casting was done in a very luxurious office space in the 7e arrondissement of Paris on the third floor. The work space was the entire floor—it was huge. The first room was very large and filled with desks and secretaries. Everyone was nice and welcoming. It was noisy and crowded. I had to walk through several rooms before I got to the manager's office. Once there, a few questions were asked but nothing fancy, mainly personal questions like: do I have children, are you married, is it okay to be far away from home for 2 weeks. Pretty unusual in my opinion, but again, I had never done something like this so I didn't know what was "normal" or not.

Of course, I took my clothes off to show them my body in my underwear. Soon after they told me I was in. I was very excited! And even more so after they told me about my paycheck. I don't recall the amount but it was so much I felt like it was indecent! Only for three days of photos in a bikini in front of the Easter Island's statues. Amazing! I felt so lucky.

There was one tiny problem: we had to leave early in the morning the next day. They were sorry about the inconvenience but there were no other options for them. I wasn't going to travel by myself, not to worry: I would travel with the staff. We would be meeting at the airport and they would give me my flight ticket then. I thought, who cares! Sometimes you need to make little sacrifices in life, for more pleasure, and for adventure.

I came home all excited and happy, with a large smile on my face. I was dancing on a pink little cloud, very high up there.

The landing was pretty harsh! My boyfriend thought that the whole thing was really weird. I was a little offended especially when he said, "Why you"? Ouch, that hurt. Did I mention Philippe was older than me? He is 12 years older than me and very down to earth. Basically he explained to me that we were in Paris, where there are a lot of famous modeling agencies. "Real" modeling agencies, with real models.

Why would a real estate company hire a girl from a porn agency and spend that kind of money on a porn actress when they could hire a professional model? Why would a real estate agency made a casting call in their office, asking the girl to strip to her underwear? Argh! He was right. It didn't make sense.

We started to look for references. I called several other agents but no one was able to give me any information. I assure you that at 9 p.m. in the days before the Internet, that wasn't easy!

Their company name was nowhere to be found. It was like they didn't exist. Then, something hit me. Why would a real estate agency take photos of a girl in front of Easter Island's statues to sell houses and apartments in France? I was confused because I was at their office! I *saw* them! *They are real, they are legit!* I didn't understand.

We decided to go back there around 10 p.m., hoping to find something to help figure this out, like a company sign. Maybe I didn't get their name right.

There was no outside sign, which isn't unusual since most of the buildings were residential apartments. We went to the third floor. Not a sign on any door, indicating a real estate company. By reflex, I pushed the door and surprisingly it wasn't locked. My heart raced. This couldn't be true. The place was empty! By empty I mean completely empty. The whole floor. Everything was gone, not even a piece of paper or a pen left on the hardwood floor. The only thing left was a light bulb in the ceiling. This was scary.

We called the cops that night. They took the whole story very seriously and took my statement. I gave them as much information and as many descriptions as I could possibly remember. They were going to go to the airport meeting at the time I was given by the so-called manager. They explained that, from what I was describing, it was obvious that it was some kind of sex trafficking organization. They had been working on some young women disappearance cases related to Chile for years. The girls would get abducted then sex trafficked into slavery.

It still gives me goose bumps even today. I was so close to leaving with them. What would have happened to me?

I kind of got an answer three months later when the police called me to come to the precinct to see if I could recognize the "manager of the real estate company." I went there and like in the movies, I recognized the guy in a line up.

I never knew what happened next but I was glad at least this one would rot in jail for a while.

The only good thing from that experience was that I started to be more careful and less trusting.

I got rid of my agent the next day. The only thing he cared about was his commission and he never did the minimum amount that an agent should do for the security of the girls that work with him—verify where he sends the girls.

That was my second agent, and he did no better than the first one. No matter what, I didn't like having an agent. All they have is a list of production companies and all they do is a few phone calls. When they don't know the production company, they don't even verify.

Taking money from girls makes me think of them as pimps.

From that day and for the rest of my career, I always found a way to work without them. The porn industry is a small world, in whatever country it may be.

Chapter 3

I KEPT WORKING A LITTLE here and there, mostly by word of mouth, and mostly in other countries like the United Kingdom, Germany, Spain, and Italy. I am not sure why I was not working in France much. Although it may have been that I was refusing scenes with sodomy. French productions rarely hired girls that wouldn't do it.

It was a business decision, once I realized how things worked—the career of a female adult performer doesn't last very long. New faces swiftly replace them. New girls are an obsession to the viewer of porn and since the adult world in Europe isn't very big I figured putting anal sex on hold for later would make my career last a little longer.

Perhaps some productions would hire me again for that "plus" I'd be offering in the future. One never knows. My goal has never been to work a lot. I didn't want it to become like just another day at the office and get bored. Doing it once in a while was a good way to enjoy it, and kept me avoiding the routine. I wanted to choose, as much as I could, when and whom I worked with, rather than do anything with anybody at any time, no matter what! I just didn't see the point, besides the monetary aspect obviously.

In between a few of these European productions, I met a great guy, a director-producer named David Caroll. He used to be a cameraman for regular French TV, and ended up in the adult industry by chance. He decided to keep doing adult movies because it was more fun and the paycheck was better.

The way he works is very friendly and fun. He is always joking, never taking it seriously. His sets always felt more like a family reunion than a porn set!

David loves everybody and everybody loves David. Once, we shot in the French Alps in winter. We drove to get there and got stuck in a blizzard. The original "one day shoot" became three, but still David managed to cook for us—every single meal. We couldn't leave the cabin and evenings were endless. This is how, gathered around the dining table, talking and joking for hours, David came up with the last name of my stage name: LORD. Until that moment I was only "Rebecca" in the movies I had already done.

At first, David was joking about my first name as he always does, since he only can remember the name of an actress if he gives her a nickname. He always found play-on-word names: he takes the end of your first name and adds some joke to it. I cannot list all the funny names he gave me that night, it's all in French anyway, but so you understand, here are examples: RebecCatastrophe. RebecCartoon. RebecCalories. RebeccaCao. RebeccaFeLate... It went on for hours. Suddenly he got tired and just asked me, "what if you add Lord to your name?" At first, I didn't understand. Where was the joke? I had no idea who Tracy Lords was, believe it or not. David explained who she was and I just became Rebecca Lord. Yeah, we just forgot there was an "s" at the end, like the silly French we are! So, to answer a question I was asked so many times in the United States—I confirm that I am not Traci Lords' sister or cousin... I'm really not!

I have met great people in this adult industry. Some of them became my friends. David is one of them. I also met horrible people. The adult industry doesn't work differently than other "civilian" business when it comes to the kind of people you run into.

Pierre Woodman is another "character" worth telling you about. In the '90s, he was one of the most famous porn directors in Europe. He is THE one who opened the porn gates between Western Europe and Eastern Europe.

Shooting in Eastern Europe before him was not an option. Adult films were made in Western Europe with Western European actresses, or in the US with US actresses. Pierre took a lot of risks (it could be really dangerous to shoot in countries like Russia) and brought back the most beautiful girls from those countries. At one point, he even went to jail because of it.

Little by little, girls from the Czech Republic, Hungary, and Russia were getting famous and some even started to build a career in Europe, like the gorgeous Tania Russof, and later in the US, the divine Silvia Saint. Pierre always took very good care of the female performers he worked with. He was always very helpful, sometimes even protective, giving advice, sending a referral for the girl so she could work with the best productions and avoid the bad ones. Today, everyone—Americans, Europeans, even Japanese—go shoot in Eastern Europe as they were doing before in Western Europe. We all owe him that.

I always liked Pierre, even if his concept of sex scenes isn't always mine. He is rather obsessed by anal sex.

I really respect the guy despite that fact he is not afraid of anything or anyone, regardless of what people might think of him. He is an ex-cop, and is a very charismatic person, seductive, honest and straightforward. He started as a photographer for a Swedish company called "Private." At the time, Private didn't shoot much video and specialized in porn books in pictures, mostly found in sex shops. Pierre explained to his boss that it would be a good idea to shoot the book stories as a video rather than just pictures, and he became THE director for the company. Private then began to shoot videos all over the world and quickly became one of the major companies of our industry. Of course, they mostly specialized in anal sex scenes. That comes from Pierre too!

They shoot all over the globe, often in very exotic places; again, thanks to Pierre. Pierre was so successful that they gave him a free pass for everything, including big budgets, so of course Pierre always found the best-looking girls and the greatest locations.

I met him in Paris. It was 1994. He heard of me, I don't know how, since I was rarely working in France and contacted me by phone. He offered me a sex scene in his next big production to be shot in Bali.

Of course, even though he charmed me over the phone, I declined since it included sodomy. Not that I have anything against it, but as I explained I was saving it for later in my career so it would last longer.

He insisted, explained that I shouldn't worry, that it would be nothing violent. I would be well taken care of. This was the typical Pierre Woodman charm that I would become used to. I politely declined and said that if it would be a "regular" scene I would gladly accept the offer.

The next day, he called back and tried to persuade me again. Before I even had time to decline, he invited me to his apartment to have a drink, and even told me to bring my boyfriend. I was speechless. Usually the producer or director has a tendency to try and get rid of the boyfriend. I didn't know what to say and sheepishly accepted to join him for a drink with my boyfriend!

We met later at his apartment in the center of Paris near the Eiffel Tower. We had a couple of drinks and then he said it was time to talk business. I answered that my decision was the same. He smiled and doubled his initial offer.

At this point I had only done a few movies, was mostly unknown even in my own country, and this kind of money represented a lot to me. As the cherry on the cake, he would bring me to the AVN show in the US and introduce me to every adult company there.

Although I was sorely tempted. I refused. I remember being very proud that I had the courage to decline.

I didn't know Pierre very well. He called back a few days later and upped the ante, again. This time I was not "that" courageous anymore.

It was a great scene as promised. I am glad I accepted even though at the time I was kind of pissed off at myself for giving way to the temptation of a fat paycheck. But in my head, a crazy idea was growing, the same crazy idea that would change my life completely and for a long time.

As I said, I was pretty much unknown in my own country, and at the time, a company called "Hot Video" was a major player in the European Adult Industry. Contrary to the name, it was not a production company but an adult magazine. Distributed in every newsstand, it was accessible to all fans. But the magazine was also the bible of the porn industry in Europe, kind of like AVN in the US. Movies were viewed and reviewed by critics, like any mainstream magazine.

For a production company, it was the holy book of who did what and with whom, to discover who was new, and what the competition was doing. For a distributor avidly reading the reviews, it told what movies to choose from. For performers, it told what companies would give him/her the best exposure. If the magazine published pictures of you, people in our business could see who you were and what you looked like.

Most of the productions would then call Hot Video to get the girl's phone number so they could hire her. Understand the process: it meant that if you didn't have any pictures published in Hot Video magazine, whether by bad luck or some photographer/journalist didn't like you, well, you remained unknown for quite some time and couldn't really work that much.

Hence the more you got your pictures published, the more publicity you had, and the quicker you became famous. Your net worth grew exponentially! You then had the luxury to choose the production you wanted to work for (or not), the male performer you wanted to work with (or not), and of course you could raise your rates accordingly.

In my opinion, this was way too much power in one entity. Basically they could decide who would succeed and who would fail. This was the game—you were in it or you were not.

Hot Video created the Hot D'or. Like the AVN Award Show in Vegas, the Hot D'Or award show was in Cannes, during the Cannes Film Festival. Pretty gutsy, don't you think? But highly clever considering that all the media on the planet was covering the Cannes Film Festival and when they had nothing better to do during the day (or night), what's better than covering the infamous Adult Show next door?

One day the phone rang and Hot Video wanted me to do a full interview with photos. Me! Not sure why so suddenly, as they ignored me for several months, but of course I said yes. When opportunities come knocking, you open the door!

So there I was, in front of the journalists, drinking a large glass of water, totally unprepared. I was really naive at the time and didn't think for one minute that I would need to prepare for an interview. We went through how and when I started doing porn movies, how old I was, and I proudly announced to them my new and recently discovered stage name!

Then one of them asked me when I lost my virginity. He dared to ask me that question! My jaw fell down like in a cartoon. I was so offended. It ripped my smile apart in an instant. *Okay, this guy is an ass*, I thought.

I wanted to protect my intimacy and dignity, so I looked him straight in the eyes and said, "It doesn't concern you, next question!"

Which was, "What are your favorite things to do in bed?"

Whaaaaaaaat???!!!

Obviously he didn't hear me the first time. What the hell was that? Now I was mad. I answered, "This is too intimate. I refuse to answer these kinds of questions." The two guys looked at each other. The one who was doing the interview remained speechless and the other one laughed his ass off then left the room.

The interview lasted 10 minutes top. I literally answered none of their questions. The first Rebecca Lord interview was the answer to the first three questions I was asked. That's it. Period.

The journalist didn't know what to do. He kept looking at his shoes. He didn't even say "nice meeting you" when I left nor did he open the door for me. He seemed glued to his chair.

The strange thing in this specific period of time is that I seemed crazy to most people who aren't in the adult industry because of this particular job, and now I looked crazy as well to the people *in* the adult industry.

Of course it didn't last very long. It got better soon enough. But I must confess that I never, to this day, like being interviewed. The worst is being interviewed on a radio show or in front of a camera.

Let's be honest. I look dumb. You think you don't like hearing your own voice on an answering machine? Ah! Try to imagine a full interview in English, which is not my mother tongue, with a French accent, then add a bunch of very smart questions like "What's your favorite position?" Since you don't have only one, you answer, "Huh….well… I don't really have one, …" "Who's your favorite actor to work with?" Since you don't want to piss off your co-workers, who *will* hear the interview one day or another, you answer, "Huh….well… I don't really have one… "Which movie are you most proud of?" Since you don't want to piss off people who hired you, knowing they *will* hear the interview some day, you answer, "Huh….well… I don't really have one…" And so on…

I have proof that I am not making this up. When you got a chance, listen carefully to Hollywood actors and actresses on TV and you will notice that when they are been interviewed about their latest movie, they all say the same thing and all sound alike: "OHHHHHH MY GOD, the director was fantastic, a pure genius, the movie is incredible, the other actors are unbelievable... blah blah blah." Well, now you know why. You're welcome.

My favorite question, and I had the pleasure to be asked this at least a hundred times: "What was the funniest moment on a set?" When you hear that question for the first time, you think really hard, smoke almost comes out of your ears. "This one I'm going to tell. I know. Wait, no… everyone can hear, that's too embarrassing for him/her... Oh, here we go. That time... wait…no… they will kill me for telling!" While you're desperately looking for an answer, the camera is still rolling. So you make little noises, to help you look smart, like "hmmmmmm" or "hehehehe" or "huh huh," then finally you end up saying, "You know what? All of them are so much fun, I don't know which one to tell you! HAHA!"

What can I say? That yesterday I slapped an actor in the face, real hard, as soon as the director yelled "action" just because I misunderstood what he wanted me to do? (When I first arrived in the US, I didn't speak English at all.)

That day, the director, Fred Lincoln, explained that it was a rehearsal and I was supposed to slap Jon Dough gently so he could lock in his shot. I had no clue what a rehearsal meant, so as usual when I didn't understand what didn't seem very important I said, "Huh huh" like I understood (how hard is it to slap someone in the face?) and when Fred yelled "action," of course I slapped him for real!

Everyone had to stop shooting for one hour because they couldn't stop laughing and because Jon's face was too red. If I said that during an interview, I would look extra-dumb, right?

Life can be odd sometimes. I was leaving Hot Video's building, angry and disappointed, when I ran into the famous photographer from Hustler magazine, James Baes. He was coming from California and just stopped by to visit Hot Video's boss. They worked together from time to time. He asked me who I was, gave me his business card, and a couple of months later I was shooting for him in Europe and ended up being one of the Hustler Honeys (cover and centerfold) in the US edition. Cherry on the cake… I made the cover of Hot Video too!

Life is full of coincidences! I love it! If I had done the full interview, I would not have met James in the elevator and I would probably not have had the life I had in the US.

Several months later, Hot Video invited me to their award show in Cannes. At the time, it was the most amazing porn "thing" I had ever been to.

This was a 24 hour award show—press conference and cocktails during the day, with dozens of photographers, journalists and cameramen, then a few scandalous starlet pictures on the "La Croisette" beach, followed by a huge award party at night, in the French tradition (elegant, lots of good wine, champagne and amazing food)!

The Hot D'Or Award Show had real shows before the actual Porn Awards. In the Hollywood tradition!

Want to hear it? I am warning you, you could die laughing! Okay, only one example then: "And…the best double penetration goooooooes toooooo…!!" I couldn't stop laughing. People were crying on stage with their little gold statue in their hands. Some of them even thanked their parents!

It was unreal.

Productions from all over the world came to that event. Their goal, besides having parties and lots of publicity internationally, was to go there for a few days, rent incredible villas right outside the city, and shoot sex scenes. Why, would you ask? Well, French Provence is beautiful and it's a real plus for production values. But mainly because they would meet actors and actresses from other countries that would have been difficult to hire or costly otherwise. They would come with performers from their own country and would kind of trade with another country's production or shoot joint productions. So basically, once a year, everyone would gather in this small city that becomes the center of the world for a few days to work and party together.

It's also the most important moment of the year for performers to find work right away and meet new companies they will work for in the future.

So I went. Philippe came along, wanting to be sure I wasn't going to get kidnapped! We were very impressed by the whole thing. I met a lot of American directors and started to shoot for them. Randy West was one of them. Ed Powers was another.

Then I met Nic Cramer. My English wasn't poor, it was just inexistent. Philippe offered to translate, and sure enough, one thing led another, and he had to translate on the set as well! He survived it but I never saw his face change colors so often in such a short time!

I felt different being around American productions. There was something distinctive about them. It was faster, well organized, straightforward and the people I worked with and worked for were all happy. Even happy to pay me! No one tried to bargain down my rates like most European companies did. It was very unusual, and it felt nice to work in a stress-free environment with people pleased to work.

Nic Cramer was also working for Private USA, among a few other companies like Sin City or Pleasure Productions. Philippe and Nic talked like they were best friends. Meanwhile I was trying to understand one or two words of their conversation. I have become quite skilled at how to pretend to understand someone, when I actually don't.

It's easy—when they look serious, do the same, and when they laugh, be ready to roll over at the exact same time they do. It works, really. Just hope they are not laughing at you, that's all!

After I worked for him in Cannes, Nic invited us to visit him in Los Angeles, anytime we wanted. He had a big house in Encino, and said we could stay there and even offered to help with whatever we would need. He would introduce me to the right production companies and tell me who to avoid, and who to work with. He explained that I could really have a nice career as an actress there.

We weren't planning to go yet, we had to think about it, but the invitation was really appealing. The United States… I dreamed about going there since I was a child. The first thing that came to my mind and way before having a "nice career in the US" was The Grand Canyon! A child's dream.

The crazy idea that was born after I had started working for Pierre Woodman was growing stronger.

A few months later, even though I didn't give much choice to Philippe about sharing the crazy life of an adult performer, Philippe and I decided to get married. It was June 1994.

It was a discreet wedding, with only a few people, mainly family and a few friends, the ones that decided not to judge me for the job I was doing. You will never guess what gift my family offered us: a honeymoon in the US!

In the back of our minds, we knew that if there was a way to make enough money so we could stay and live there, we would. What did we have to lose? Nothing. Quite the opposite—a new life and for me the chance to work with professional people that love their work and do it well, far from the complicated shoots in Europe, stress on the sets, never knowing what would happen next. The only question that remained: are we going to like the United States as much as we thought we would?

Chapter 4

WE ARRIVED IN LOS ANGELES. Nic Cramer came to pick us up. We hugged him and jumped in his 1976 black Corvette and headed to the Valley via the 405 freeway.

My sleepy eyes were already impressed by the size of the highway. Where were all the small and medium size cars? The sun was up high, and we were driving fast. We spoke in English and it felt like a song to my ears during the entire drive. I was feeling good, really good.

Nic gave us the big tour—the Hollywood sign, Beverly Hills, Sunset Boulevard, all the clichés I'd seen on TV or in the movies. It was like a dream.

We stopped for lunch before we got to his house. We went to a place called "Jerry's Deli" on Ventura Boulevard. I wasn't very hungry because of the jet lag, so I ordered a Cobb salad, thinking, "I'll just chew on two tomatoes, to be polite." It may sound weird to you that I could remember what I ordered more than 20 years ago, but it was my first meal in the US, and what the waiter brought me was a plate that could literally feed 5 French people!!

So here I was, holding my free refill (I had no idea what that meant at the time) iced tea glass in the air... cheers and welcome to L.A.!

Nic's house was in a very nice area called Encino Hills. The place looked like it came out of an episode of the TV show *Desperate Housewives*. Very "family oriented!" Except no one ever knocked on his front door to offer him a pie! Instead they sent cops knocking, once in a while, for no reason.

Every neighbor was probably aware of what Nic was doing for a living. The way they ignored me or the look they would throw at me when I would say "hi" was self-explanatory enough. I'm surprised their kids didn't wear a mask with Nic's face on it for Halloween.

The house was huge with many empty bedrooms. Nic had two roommates: Keith, a guitar player in a Rock band, and Christy (AKA: Shelby Stevens) an adult performer.

Keith was the kind of person people would call "a peace and love dude." His blond hair all the way down to his butt, he smoked pot all day, loved everyone and his social mind was set on what belongs to you belongs to me, and what belongs… to you, belongs to me!!!!

Christy was very nice. Typical California looking girl—blonde with large breasts, wearing cute shorts or sweat pants around the house. We got along great except that my boxer puppy was always chewing up her dildos!

Sadly, I think the boxer puppy I got a couple months later made our relationship a little cloudy. Even though he behaved around the house and didn't chew on stuff, he had a thing for Christy's dildo collection. She would hide them but my devilish puppy, Beavis (named after the cartoon character), would always find a way to get to them. I guess he thought that her dildos were fun toys! Which isn't exactly wrong!

For the 4th of July, Nic threw a huge party at his place. Of course most of his guests were from the adult industry. "Great opportunity for you to meet people," he said.

I always suspected that he threw such a big party for us. Not that we were special or anything, but that's just the way he is, proud to be helpful. Of course he would have thrown a party anyway, but probably a smaller version of it.

I did meet a lot of people. I can't tell you who they were, simply because not being able to have a conversation with people truly doesn't help getting to know them and remembering them. How frustrating. I remind you that at the time I was not speaking a word of English.

Although, I did remember two of them: Steven St Croix, a male performer who came to introduce a beautiful and adorable blonde doll named Jenna Jameson. At the time, she was "only" a model for adult magazines and wanted to do her "debut" in the porn industry. What struck me was that Jenna knew already exactly what she wanted—to be an exclusive contract girl and the biggest porn star of all time. That was her condition to becoming an adult actress. Take it or leave it. As we all know, she succeeded and a lot more.

AFTER THE PARTY, I had to think more about how would I start getting jobs and less about how great I felt being in the US. For the exact same reasons that I had none in France, I really hated the idea of having an agent in Los Angeles. But it would make things way more complicated than where I came from. The adult industry in the US isn't quite the same size! You could compare it to the Cobb Salad experience at Jerry's Deli.

I guess it's proportioned to the country size. Back then seven movies were being shot per day, just in California. That's a lot of productions, and a lot of talent!

I am not sure exactly how many were shot in France every day but I wouldn't be surprised that seven was the number of movies shot in one month! I'm talking about professional movies, not amateur.

Some US talent agencies had hundreds of performers. When a production called to see who would be available, the agent probably recommended whoever popped into his mind or who was physically in his office at the time of the call.

Needless to say, when you first start, being in the agent's office all day helped a lot.

There was no way I could do this. It sounded like begging to me. Add the fact that I've never been the patient type. I just decided to take the risk and do it without an agent.

My plan was to go to every major production and introduce myself to everyone. Nic helped me a lot and gave me a list of the main production companies, the most famous and active ones, along with a list of male performers he would recommend working with, as a start. I would make up my own mind as I went along.

This was incredibly helpful. We quickly became good friends with Nic. He was genuinely generous, sincere, and never asked anything in return. To this day, Nic Cramer is still one of my best friends.

I swiftly realized there was one thing that needed to be done as fast as possible. I had to learn English. This needed to be take care of not only for my job, but also for my everyday life. I have many examples of how it was affecting me. I actually washed my hair every day for ten long days with a body lotion because I couldn't read the label! I am sorry to say that during all that time I really thought American hair conditioners sucked.

So I started to watch TV with subtitles like an addict. Keith and I became couch potato buddies watching a lot of cartoons. I found out that pot and cartoons is a never ending love story, and I followed the O.J. Simpson's trial like a real fan. His lawyers kind of became my English teachers.

I spent my days knocking on adult companies' doors and meeting their managers. They all had one thing in common. They looked and acted like successful managers from any other industry, only the posters on their office walls were different.

Unlike the French, the Americans run the adult industry like they would run any other business. The content itself is a detail, the numbers their motivation. They wanted money, plain and simple. And of course, like in any business taken seriously, a good product needs good marketing. Everything has to be marketed and the choice of performers is golden—the box cover of a movie is so important. It may sound logical to you, but it wasn't to me then. I was learning.

Hollywood is an incredible machine that was made to create stars. They created a star system, a powerful marketing machine that doesn't exist anywhere else. Even if the adult industry is a way smaller version, the system remained the same in the '90s.

I loved it. It was fair and square, straightforward. This system meant there was much more respectful behavior towards the actors in general. Just imagine your boss telling you that without you he would simply not exist! That the whole business itself would not exist!

Not bad, huh? Even if it applies to any country in the world (that technically without porn performers, porn would not exist), the US was the only place I have been that made me feel that way. No more French "amateur look alike" box covers. I was more than ready to play the game.

FIRST THINGS FIRST. As a "product," my priority was to act like one. Let's start with my rates— as we all know, the higher a price is for a product, the more people think it's really worth it. So I wasn't going to sell myself cheap and would try to choose whom I worked for carefully.

The people I met seemed to like me. I was a new face with a different look and a French accent. As far as I could see, there were opportunities, so I put my trip to the Grand Canyon on standby. I already believed I would stay in the US with my husband, for quite some time.

I started working for Randy West, Ed Powers, Anabolic, etc…all the main pro-am companies with good reputations. This was the same way a lot of newcomers did in the '90s. These guys were famous for having newcomers: it was their signature. There was no comedy or dialogue, no story line, just straight to sex. We called them "vignettes."

No matter what, I couldn't have worked for sophisticated big productions at the time, being incapable of pronouncing one phrase that made sense, as I still was not understanding any English at all.

The list of actors Nic Cramer gave me worked pretty well. Eleven names were on it. One thing I didn't expect: that I would piss off the ones who weren't on that list. After a couple of months I already had the reputation of been a pretentious person at best.

Sometimes, reputations are built on irrelevant little things mixed together. Chatter increases them gradually and in no time it's ten times worse than the original chatter. In my case, I had people saying that I was expensive and… French!

I had to admit that when you put things together, I can't blame them. Happily that didn't last too long.

Only one actor hated my guts for many years. But he was crazy and he hated everybody anyway. The guy almost punched me in the face on a set for no reason at all.

It isn't difficult to get to know all the actors after a while. That isn't the case with the girls since they are so many of them, and some of them just come and go and only stick around for a few months. Successful actors stay for a very long time, 10 to 40 years even. They work all the time, every day, 7 days a week.

I can picture some of you thinking, "Wow, dream work!" No, no, and no! Don't think with your penis but with your brain. I apologize for breaking down your fantasy, but most adult actors don't have a private life. They simply can't. The uneven schedule. Knowing what time they start but never when they will be done. Plus, and most importantly, having a girlfriend is no easy task. They need to be in shape and keep their sexual stamina for the camera. Add the fact that having a "civilian" girlfriend that would accept that kind of job is quite complicated. It's a pretty lonely life.

Lots of them end up with female performers because they do the same job and they will be understood. Still, it's difficult for a couple in the adult industry to last very long.

As for the performance itself, let me be clear: they don't all have sex with actresses they are attracted to! It's not like they pick them. The production does. It is hard work, especially for the guys. When the camera is rolling, positions are chosen to be visual, not to be comfortable or enjoyable. Some positions they make us do are even out of this world. A cartoonist would not make his character do half these things! We, as performers, make you believe it's all nice, fun and smooth. In reality, sometimes 20 mosquitoes are attacking us during the most intimate moments. Which is always when my line comes up: "Oh James, keep going. Fuck me harder, I love it."

We have sex in extreme conditions sometimes. It's our job, whether it's 125 degrees or 25! Our job is your fantasy.

I also need to remind you that that little blue pill, Viagra, didn't exist at the time. It makes the job a little easier for male performers nowadays. But it also means other problems. Viagra will make you hard, it is true, but sometimes it makes it harder to get off, which obviously is a problem for a male performer.

In my first year in the US, I did several scenes outside. One of them was for Private, out in the sun, on the hottest day in Los Angeles since 1890. Ian Daniels, the actor I was working with fainted. He had sunstroke.

That same year in Winter I was shooting on top of a building's roof in downtown L.A. at night. This time I was working for Cameron Grant. It was the "coldest weather in 50 years," they said. Don't get me wrong, I am not complaining about the fever I got after both scenes. I am just saying that the actor (Nick East, in this case) couldn't use the weather as an excuse for not getting it up. Because it's not an option! His job is to perform no matter what and for the time needed.

Now you understand why only a handful of performers are trustworthy and why adult productions only use the same ones over and over.

My first big movie, meaning a high budget movie with artwork and a script, was for Nic Cramer, a little earlier than that L.A. roof scene. On top of being one of the leads in the movie, Nic made me his makeup artist as well. One of my scenes was in a junkyard at night, with Dick Nasty. I remember finishing at 6AM. That night, the crew was wearing winter clothes: gloves, scarves, coats... Nic provided us with huge heaters in between cuts, but we were still freezing. He finally took some of his clothes off, for the time being, to show compassion and solidarity. I had never seen a director that did this during my entire career.

Kaitlyn Ashley was the lead character in the movie, she played the Malcolm McDowell character and I was one of her crazy gang members. We were all wearing white clothing and a black hat. I was the one breaking all kind of things. I loved breaking things. It was fun! If it rings a bell, that's because it was a spoof of the movie *A Clockwork Orange*.

But our movie title was much more attractive. It was *A Clockwork Orgy*! You wouldn't believe how many porn parodies have been made over the years. Let me give you a few samples: *Porn on the 4th of July, Sex Trek, the Next Penetration, The Da Vinci Load, Splatman, American Booty, Penetrator*, and so on…

I thought it was fun playing characters that I knew from mainstream movies. I got to be Keanu Reeves from *The Matrix*, Lara Croft, and a few others. But the funniest one was a cute girl coming out from a TV set, to have sex with Butthead, from *Beavis and Butthead*.

Tony Tedeschi was dressed and made up to look like the cartoon character. Needless to say that wasn't sexy at all. Tony was a huge fan of the cartoon. He was extremely credible playing his part, which made the whole thing hilarious. One thing he liked to do was whisper in my ear French words that sounded sexy to him, only he had no idea what they meant. "Mon petit Camembert" (my little French stinky cheese), for example! It really didn't turn me on, I don't know why!

That scene was made for a Buck Adams movie. Buck was seriously sick that day and couldn't direct the scene. Instead of canceling it, Tony being all made up and stuff, we decided to shoot it ourselves. Even though performers are not cameramen or directors, being on the set often gives us a pretty good idea of what needs to be done. We had so much fun and laughed so hard, it took us hours to shoot the scene but it is one of the very best memories I have. That day I promised myself that I would direct a movie one day.

Nic was very demanding about his dialogue and acting skills. Very rare are the actors that can pull that off, and Kaitlyn was one of the few. I know most people who watch adult films fast forward the dialogue to go straight to what's interesting to them: sex. I would surely do the same if I were you. Why would anyone buy a porn movie to watch people having a conversation? Or should I say, trying to look like they are having a conversation, not just repeating their lines.

Adult performers are performers, not actors. We are known for being terrible at it—it's a fact. Some people are naturally gifted (like Sasha Grey), but it really isn't the majority. One thing needs to be said on our behalf: it's not really our fault.

Being an actor isn't something you are born with. Real actors go to school. They work on their craft. The so-called "scripts" are handed to us at the last minute on a set. If it's only two or three lines, we can live with it, but when it's three pages long with only a half hour to learn it all, let's be honest. We simply cannot pull it off! We went to the Sex University classroom not to the Actor's Studio!!

Philippe and I met David Cimini on Nic's set during *A Clockwork Orgy*. He was a freelance journalist/photographer for several adult magazines. He specialized in news, events and gossip. Dave had another job too—he was a member of the paparazzi.

He was known for taking pictures of porn stars with famous people from the real world such as Hollywood actors, rock stars and so on. This wasn't too difficult to do considering the opportunity of being in L.A. where all the parties happen and the constant attraction between porn and Hollywood. Anyhow, Dave was a very busy man, too busy, and he couldn't handle everything by himself anymore. So he thought of Philippe to give him a hand. My husband was a photographer for a little while, in France, a long time before I met him and was looking for more work. It was the perfect opportunity for both David and him. They worked together for a long time. Philippe covered the adult industry and David had more time to focus on his paparazzi business.

After two years, Philippe took over, as David was too busy with his paparazzi agency, and worked for several foreign magazines, mainly Japanese and French. It was weird to run into him on various movie sets he was covering for the magazines. At first, he would avoid my scenes, which I understand completely, but then the French magazine he worked for was not too happy about it. Me being French and starring in US movies, they wanted the coverage. We learned to work together after some long talks. Wasn't easy at all for a while.

My only experience as a model was in France, for *New Look* and *Hustler* magazines. I was far from realizing how big the adult magazine industry was in the US. I didn't realize that one day I would be featuring dance on the road in strip clubs and that I would need the "celebrity" that magazines bring you. I started to add to my list of "doors needing to be knocked at" a few photographers. Suzy Randall was one of the first.

This great English lady was shooting for everyone in the US and internationally too. Photography was her life. She started as a model and photographed herself for *Playboy*. Yeah, she is that good! Suze shot me right away. She used to call me her little Froggy in front of everyone! In six years' time, being in L.A., she shot me 19 times.

You must realize that, in the '90s, it was very rare for girls from Europe to come to L.A. Of course, some did, but it was always a very short period of time. My looks were just different from the typical California blonde: brunette, skinny, no tats, no piercings, I was all natural. It was always a real plus for me during my entire career. AVN called me "The French Pastry."

Layouts were fun. I enjoyed doing it a lot. Photography magnifies femininity. All my experiences with nude photographers went well. Well, all but one.

I can't really talk about Earl Miller since we never got the chance to work together. After meeting with him, a few days later, I went to a cocktail party thrown by an erotic TV network called Spice Chanel. He was there as well and came up to me with two glasses in his hand, and obviously one of them was for me. Except, I didn't recognize the guy! I still don't know what came to my mind that day, but I vividly remember mistaking him for an annoying fan. I refused the champagne and looked at him like, if he was going to step closer to me, I was going to rip his eyes out. Never heard from him again! I really blew it that day! This was one of my biggest regrets.

One I can talk about is Carl Walker. He was mainly working for Penthouse at the time. Dyanna Lauren and I were called to do a girl/girl photo shoot for Penthouse, photographed by Carl Walker. I was a mummy. My entire body and face were wrapped in a large band. Only my eyes and the entrance of my nose were spared.

The story line was that Dyanna was supposed to discover me, free me and be turned on by me. At the beginning of the shoot I needed to be strapped in the air, attached to the ceiling. Fine with me. I didn't mind staying in the air for a few minutes… unless everyone leaves for lunch break, forgetting I am up there! That's exactly what they did.

I couldn't scream, couldn't move and I could hear them talking and laughing in the other room. If I had had a fight with my husband, I would have thought he had paid someone for some vicious revenge. But we did not.

Almost a half an hour later, I heard my dear and lovely colleague scream like someone killed her cat in front of her: "OH MY GOD, OH NO, REBECCAAAAAA!!!!" Yes, "Hi, don't worry, I didn't go anywhere…" I won't go into details about how the rest of the shoot went, since my ego was badly hurt for the rest of the day. Surprisingly, *Penthouse* loved the result.

AROUND THAT SAME TIME I lost my virginity to a girl. My first time was on screen, nothing fancy about it, since most of us are young when we decide to join the Porn Academy! It is quite common that performers have their first "something" in front of a camera.

My scene was with Felicia and I was so very lucky! She was well known for being a 200% lesbian, which helped quite a bit. She quickly made me feel comfortable. She guided me and was very sweet. The worst thing that could have happened to me was to have a partner who never experienced it as well, or even worst, doesn't like girls but pretended to. It happened several times through the years!

In the '90s, girl/girl scenes were very popular and the productions made tons of them, which explains why a lot of female performers were doing lesbian scenes even though they didn't like it.

I find it pathetic if you ask me. They were so many other ways to make money and enjoy your job. Having sex with a girl that doesn't like touching you and is only doing it for the money makes you feel dirty. It's almost humiliating. Of course, you can sense when a partner is disgusted by you and is forcing herself into doing it. It happened to me several times and I hated it. Now, as a producer/director, when I contact a girl to work for me, I always insist that she tells me the truth about being into girls or not. It really shows on the screen when one of the girls is really not into lesbian sex.

Anyway, my first experience was great and very enjoyable although I thought I was not really into girls. Thanks to Felicia, I discovered something I didn't know was in me. Of course, sex in front of a camera is not sex in private and it really depends on your partner in most cases. It is quite difficult to truly enjoy yourself when you hear "cut" pretty often. You then have to stop whatever it is you were enjoying doing. Frustrating. So let's just say that if my first lesbian experience was truly great and enjoyable, I still hadn't experience it in my private life.

Several weeks later, for my birthday, Nic Cramer organized a big party and Felicia came out of my birthday cake! You know, one of those monster cakes where you can hide a person inside.

The party was great and I was having a lot of fun. The beautiful and sexy Felecia was there, in the comfort of my own home. That day I truly discovered lesbian sex.

It is because of that moment that I kept doing girl/girl scenes for many years. Felecia was my coming out, of some sort! To this day, I am not sure if the term bi-sexual is accurate for me, as I still prefer sex with men. I have never considered myself a lesbian but I had memorable experiences in that domain.

Chapter 5

WHILE THE ADULT INDUSTRY in France does their annual meeting during the Summer time (Hot d'Or), the Americans do theirs in Las Vegas, in January. You may have heard of the Consumer Electronic Show (C.E.S), one of the biggest conventions in the world. Well, for years ours was next door during the exact same period. Sometimes it was even in the same hotel and casino. Lots of fans were always jumping from one convention to another.

For my first time at the convention, I was invited by Anabolic Productions to do their promotion. Most productions have a booth on the convention floor and an actress standing there, taking photos with fans and signing autographs. The way things work is no different from any other convention. The companies' goal is to meet buyers, distributors, stores, and so on coming from all over the US or from all over the world, to sell their rights to other countries or exchange products. It is also open to the public and of course the fans.

What a zoo! I had never been to a place like that before and never have, ever since. I remember getting to the front door at 9 a.m. so I could arrive at my booth around 9:50. It was so ridiculously crowded. I had to fight my way in to get there! On the way to the booth, if you ran into someone you knew, you had to wave your arms up in the air and scream, "Hiiiiiiii, I will see you later!!" knowing, of course, you probably will never see him/her again. Trying to find anybody on the convention floor is like trying to find a small Cobb Salad at Jerry's Deli!

As for the fans, they always find a way to catch up with you, somehow, and have their autographs signed, wherever your stand might be or wherever you are on the convention floor. I wonder how!

At last, once you are physically inside the booth, safe and sound, one thing comes to mind and occupies your thoughts. "Don't drink anything all day!" Getting to the toilets of the convention floor is the trickiest of all. They are usually next to the bar. Getting from your booth to the bar is a constant fight! You are trying to hide as much as possible, but you get grabbed by fans wanting to get a picture with you every ten feet. You meet company people that want to work with you and "Why not talk about it now?" People want to introduce you to other people and "Why not get a drink if you're heading that way?" Finally, there are people at the bar that want to offer you a drink and talk about anything, or there are journalists/photographers from the press that want you to show some boobies. "Get real, Rebecca, it's an adult convention after all." When you finally reach the toilets, and you can't hold it anymore, there is a huge line and you have to wait forever, and guess what—you can't hide anymore!

As a performer, this convention wasn't something you could advoid if you intended to make a career. It was the best way to show you existed. For the professionals, which is obvious, but also for the fans. I said earlier that the porn industry wouldn't exist without talent. One other thing is for sure. It also wouldn't exist if there weren't any fans buying your movies.

In fact, movies and magazines' content are based mostly on what the viewers like and want. It is not the other way around. It's basic supply and demand 101.

To get the best exposure possible, the game was to do as many interviews as possible during the convention time. I would also need to go to parties at night. If my feet still carried me, I could even go to two or three different ones per night. Not because it's fun, although some of them were, but again, for the purpose of showing yourself, getting exposure and meeting people for future jobs.

I met a French photographer from Hot Video with whom Philippe and I became friends later on. Laurent moved to the US and pretty quickly went off on his own. He became Laurent Sky and as of today he is still very active in the business. He is a very talented photographer, with a huge imagination. Also a funny person that always put people in a good mood on sets. Curiously, we only worked one time together, on a photo shoot, and it was for a box cover for one of the movies I directed.

I met a lot of people, mostly at night, during the numerous parties. During one of these parties, I met an interesting person. He seemed very different from the others. He was quite polite and discreet, everyone seemed to know him. His name was Momo. This Japanese reporter was welcomed everywhere he went.

He was always wearing a smile on his face, and was extremely respectful to the girls and they loved him. As for the productions and distributors, since Momo was the only official connection to Japan, they all wanted his attention. Momo was almost American. He was in the US one month out of every two, covering events and movies, and did it for many years. We got along well and we saw each other many times after that. Even if we never became real friends, he trusted me enough to take me to Japan.

It was amusing to watch my colleagues' faces at their booths, after a few days of non-stop craziness. We were all dressed up in a provocative way, some of the girls were even in their underwear all day, and we all had one thing in common—our feet couldn't bare one more minute of those porn high heels! The most courageous girls were posing in front of their booth but most of us were hiding our bare feet behind our counters, where no one could see them. Since then, I always wondered what newscasters on TV are wearing from the waist down.

Next to my bare feet, I displayed 2 boxes. One for business cards and the other one for fake business cards given by wanna-be producers/photographers. Imagine how easy it is for some people to try and make you believe they are in the adult industry and hand out business cards around in a place like this! It might work sometimes with newbies but very quickly you figure it out by asking questions. Sometimes the guy was really good at it and I would have doubts, but then I would just ask which girls he shot and then a few phone calls would be enough to realize I dealt with a liar.

The thing is, I couldn't tell them straight to their faces, "I know you're one of these wannabes! Got you! Ahah!" I had to be respectful as much as I could, because I represented the company that paid me to be there. So the best way I found to deal with this was to listen to their speeches and politely look like I would keep their business cards, then I would put them in box number two. In box number one I kept the real cards.

I was so tired after a while, my brain was malfunctioning and I shredded a guy's business card to pieces right in front of him, promising I would call him as soon as I got back home! The wanna-be producer insisted that I wouldn't and I insisted back that I would, not understanding why he looked so upset.

On the last day of the convention there was, of course, the AVN Award Show. This was very similar to the French Hot D'Or. Same type of people crying on stage, only in a fancier and bigger theatre.

I went back to the AVN/CES convention every year. It was always a unique experience, with different production companies to sign for, and once I got used to it, I actually really liked the whole zoo thing. Everyone was always in a good mood and seemed happy to reunite there once a year.

The fact that the show happened in one of my favorite cities, Las Vegas, also helped tremendously to face the days of really hard work in high heels, the toilet line and so on.

The way Las Vegas works never ceases to amaze me. It is just an incredible city. The first time I got there was by car, at night. Half an hour before I arrived, I could see the bright lights in the sky over the highway. I even thought that the state line was Vegas; all those neon signs and lights. I was blown away when I finally reached Sin City! Nothing can prepare you for Las Vegas, no films or pictures. You have to be there to live it, to realize how grand it is. I have travelled a lot in my life and have never seen anything even close to it. It's beautiful (in its own way), powerful, crazy and unique…and…not too far away from the Grand Canyon!

Chapter 6

It was time for me to do the trip to the Grand Canyon. I couldn't wait any longer. I had read so many books, had seen so many pictures and postcards.

We went back to L.A., packed a bag with t-shirts, shorts and sunscreen and off we went. Our car wasn't what you would call a fancy car. Let's just say it had a roof and a motor that supposedly ran okay, which wasn't the case for the heater or AC.

I had a very strange feeling when the map I was holding indicated that we were only few miles away and it was freezing outside. Because of our bad heater it was cold inside the car as well. Then came the snow. It seemed that the roads were closed!

Well it was winter after all! How naïve of us not to have thought about it. The thing is that in all the pictures, you always see the Grand Canyon under the sun, with silly tourists wearing hats and sunglasses. Ignorant French people like us thought the desert were always warm! Philippe drove for hours trying to find an access road, until a snowstorm buried our tiny hope of seeing anything.

On the way back, we ran into an old wood sign saying, "Grand Canyon." I courageously got out of the car with my little summer crop top and I posed next to the sign. Philippe took a picture of the only thing that proves we were there! As a result, the picture was all white but you could still see the black sunglasses I had on.

After a few months in L.A, I started to get busy and adult companies began to trust me more and more with dialogue. The first director who really took a risk giving me dialogue was Fred Lincoln who I mentioned before with the Jon Dough slap story.

Often, but not always, when dialogue is an important part of a porn movie, it means a higher budget, which logically is handled by high-end directors from the most successful companies. Vivid, VCA, Sincity, Wicked Pictures... After a few months, I worked for all of them, including erotic networks like the Playboy Channel or Spice Network.

I was busy but I could have been busier. I just didn't want to burn out my career too fast. If you are seen too much in a short period of time, people get tired of you. Refusing work is a tough thing to do sometimes but I thought it was necessary. Plus, and so very importantly, I needed to keep my private life safe and sound. What does that mean? Other than the obvious: spending quality time with your loved ones or having enough time on your hands to do the stuff that you enjoy in life, like going to the movies three times a week, taking care of my dogs, and having a nice dinner with my husband or some friends.

Basically, having a normal life, outside of the adult industry. In my opinion, leaving your work at your doorstep is the best thing to do to keep your sanity. If you let your job take control of your personal life and do not build an imaginary fence to protect it, this industry will eat you alive.

You easily lose track of the real world, and the "big porn family" becomes your only family. It is fine to go to a party with your co-workers once in a while but not all the time. The porn industry has no limit. It solicits you 24/7, if you let it.

The thing is, most people feel obligated. They are afraid that if they lose touch with the adult world for an instant, they may miss something important.

Some girls even feel obligated to have sex with a director or a producer. I can assure you that, if there is a business where you *don't* need to sleep with someone to get the job, it's the porn industry!

No couch promotion either! You, as the talent, are a good selling product or you aren't. Your performance has been screened, reviewed and judged. There is no space for hypocrisy, and certainly no need to try and climb the ladder that way.

You're either a bad product, a medium product, a good product or a best-selling product. What they call "bankable" in Hollywood. Plain and simple.

Think about it—wouldn't it be wonderful to have everything in your life so clear and simple?

I do! I actually find that state of mind a very healthy one. Yes, you read right. I'm saying that I think, in theory, the porn industry has a healthy state of mind. Here, I say it again: healthy, healthy, healthy!

I have heard so many negative things about our industry. Some are true of course (as true as it would be in any other industry for that matter), but keep in mind that they are mainly said by people outside of the adult industry, people that have no idea what's behind the green door.

Of course there are drugs. I believe losing track of reality is one of the main reasons why some use. I am just saying that a lot of people use. I might add that I have never, in 20 years, had anyone walk up to me and propose hard drugs or try to influence me in any way (except for one person, in Europe). Most of the people taking drugs in the adult industry are very discreet about it. In the '90s most of us wouldn't have treated it with such benevolence. It was just a matter of respecting the other people that work with you.

Too much pressure, being out of touch with the real world, living a crazy life, being young and naïve—it is a bad cocktail and when mixed with drugs it can be lethal. Either you won't last long or your life turns to hell. A few performers committed suicide. Some I knew, some I didn't, and some I knew very well. Hell, I even had sex with some, and several times. Then you wake up one day and they are gone forever, without a warning. What a mess.

The little girl lost syndrome.

Forget the porn industry for a second. A young pretty girl (or boy), coming from a small town, by herself, to a big city gets rich and famous too quickly. Sound familiar?

A perfect anti-example—our dear Ron Jeremy. Nothing seems to ever affect or change him. It is funny as hell that my favorite New Yorker has surfed the adult industry wave since the '70s without a scratch. Everyone loves having Ron around. He is a comedian and always has good stories to tell. Wherever you go with him, he has everyone's attention and he loves it. Ron has so much charisma. Talk shows or any kind of events, he is the best host you can have.

We hosted an event in a strip club together once. He led the stage the entire time, I just had to follow him. The microphone and I aren't best friends, as you know. This was such a relief to have Ron doing it all!

Now, having said that, I am done having lunch with him. I did once, but never again. It's just impossible to eat with him or have a conversation. Ron Jeremy is more famous than the President. As soon as you sit down, people recognize him and come from everywhere to talk to him and ask for autographs. And Ron being Ron, nice and talkative, he takes the time to sign autographs for everyone, make jokes... while you're trying to eat your lunch. When finally he had a few minutes to spare, he fell asleep right in front of my eyes!

This was so unexpected and so weird. I just didn't know what to do. At first, I thought he was playing with me. "Haha, very funny Ron!" Then I got seriously worried. Panic must had shown on my face because some people I have never seen before in my life, sitting two tables across from ours, said, "Oh, you don't know?!" (Like I am some idiot.) "Ron Jeremy is narcoleptic, just be patient, and he'll wake up!" Me (with a complicit smile): "Oh yeah I know! Thanks!" I finished my coffee slowly, looking through the window, even faked having some more liquid in my cup for a bit, and I waited…

Although Ron is the sweetest person in the whole world, he was not on my list of performers to work with. Has nothing to do with the great human being he is. It's simply a matter of my taste when it comes to men!

He doesn't always fall asleep, trust me. Of course, he had, numerous times, tried to arrange a sex scene with me through various companies. I always denied. We kept meeting on several sets and he knows I won't have sex with him. It's no big deal between us.

Chapter 7

ONE YEAR HAD PASSED. It was time for us to move out of Nic's house. The little birds were ready to fly away from their nest! Honestly, we just needed some more privacy. Too many people there, all the time, that came and went. Nic likes to have many roommates and at one point it was just too many people around (he was even doing his casting at the house). There was nothing unusual about wanting to have our own place. So we did.

Around that same time, something happened that was going to change my professional life forever. While we were still at Nic's, one night, I received a phone call from a set photographer named Rick Christmas, a man with whom I became inseparable only a couple of months later. His voice over the phone sounded nervous and he stammered something like, "Please, tell me they are wrong, tell me it isn't true!" I couldn't understand what he was talking about. After he calmed down, he explained to me that he had been on a movie set for the last 2 hours or so, and that everyone was talking about the Frenchy (my nickname at the time) being HIV positive.

Between people gossiping the info and the fact that I got tested for it only a day before, and didn't have the results back yet, I got scared instantly. What if they found out about it before I did? Is that even possible that the lab released my results without consulting me first? My heart started pumping real fast and my eyes were tearing up. The clinic that handled most of all adult performers' HIV tests was closed already.

I couldn't speak on the phone. My legs were shaky. I was probably very pale. I hung up the phone and then I turned around to look at my husband. Suddenly it hit me. I realized what I may have done, how selfish I had been for over a year and a half. What I might have done TO HIM.

Five more people called me that night. Rick, David Cimini and Nic decided to make some phone calls to find out what was going on exactly. What was real and what was gossip.

They found out that it wasn't me. It was someone else's nightmare. But it could just as easily have been mine. Barbara Doll, another French performer, was in town for a few weeks, and people mixed up the two of us. The clinic had leaked the info about the "French girl" and minutes later, radio-gossip said Rebecca Lord was HIV positive.

I think that the porn industry offers a secure work environment for the performers to work in the safest health conditions. The main reason being that the performers are professionals and have sexual intercourse with each other, in front of other professionals. They get tested for HIV and STDs every 3 weeks. Unfortunately, back in the early '90s, it was once every three months.

Does it mean we're safe? Absolutely not! It means two things: 1. The adult companies cover their asses from the government. 2. This "system" gives a sense of false security and comfort so the performers who feel safe "party" with anybody.

Do you really believe for one second that actors and actresses never have sex with "civilians" outside of the industry? What if my partner "did it" the night before, "uncovered" with a person at risk, and I had sex with him (or her) the next day on a set?! The negative HIV test presented to me from 2 weeks earlier doesn't mean much anymore.

I know that most performers are responsible people and are very careful when it comes to sex outside the business. Unfortunately, one careless person is enough to put the whole industry in jeopardy.

"The black list," "AIDS scare," or "HIV outbreak"; those are words I heard too often over the past years.

"The black list" is a list of performer names that have been, directly or indirectly, in sexual contact with someone that has been found HIV positive (or in the best case scenario, contracted a STD).

The "AIDS scare" is what follows. People freaking out, including production companies, and it's mostly decided that everyone is now wearing condoms... until time does what it does best: "flies!" Then people forget. Everything is back to normal as if nothing happened. Business as usual. Until another "HIV outbreak." I have heard many things about the adult industry HIV outbreaks. People like to gossip about it. Including the press. It probably makes them feel more secure in the comfort of their civilian life.

As it was said about our industry being like any other business, I would say that the porn industry also reflects the "clichés" of our society. It's like the plane being the safest way of transportation. No matter what, it sometimes crashes.

For the very few that were known to be HIV positive, they mostly disappeared from the adult industry. No one talks about them; it must bother us somehow. I wonder how they are doing today.

There was an actor I worked with several times, the first year I was in the US. His stage name was Marc Wallice. He was HIV positive and kept working for a year, using a fake HIV test (and without condoms, of course).

I deeply would like to express what I feel about him but I won't. I don't want this book to be one of those score settling books, or call it: "Porn, the Revenge." Seriously, I think revealing his name is plenty, and let's just add that sometimes, I am not strong enough to forget, let alone to forgive.

I wish these HIV outbreak would cease once and for all. I strongly think that condoms are the only way to keep everybody safe. I heard people from our industry saying that it is up to the performers to work with or without it and that the State of California or the government should not regulate it. I mostly agree with that statement. Performers are responsible enough to know what they should or shouldn't do. Although the past years have demonstrated that it doesn't work, hence the AIDS scares once in a while.

However, if we come back to my "plane example," the adult industry has auto-regulated itself fairly good considering.

As for my long and scary evening, at the end, I was almost relieved. I would still have to go back to the clinic and do another test like everybody else though. I remind you that at the time, it was Elisa testing, not DNA, and it took a few days to get the results. The consequence for me was that I hated myself for being one of those people who think drama only happened to others.

When the final negative results came back from the clinic, I then took the decision that I will *never ever* work without condoms again. No exceptions.

I was going to lose some jobs surely. Most companies would not hire me probably. I truly didn't care at all. There was not enough money in the world for such a risk. I don't even understand how stupid I was to never think about it for the past year and a half I worked without condoms.

I needed a brain and needed it now!

Chapter 8

IN THE '90S, most actresses had a Fan Club. We were still using regular mail at the time (if you are under 20 years old and are reading this, mailing a letter required a piece of paper, a pen, an envelope and a stamp). I started mine in a very modest and simple way: by subscription, selling photos, magazines, VHS videotapes and Polaroids.

A Polaroid was a big deal back then. It was an instant camera, where film would pop out right after you took it. Back before digital cameras they were all the rage.

I read every single letter myself, and little by little, I learned to know who were these people that we called "fans." Of course every person is different, but let's try grouping them in four main categories, to simplify.

The "classic" fan. Clear and simple, we know why he's here and what he wants. Depending on his impulse and sexual urge, he contacts you irregularly and his orders are always the same: uneven.

The "addict" fan. He follows you and knows everything about you (sometimes even more than you do about yourself. I kid you not). For instance, he knows publications, reviews or movie titles you're not even aware of yet. He buys everything that there is to buy and writes to know how you are doing very often. Careful! There is a line not to cross—you don't want him to become the stalker fan!

The lonely fan. Loneliness is too personal for me to have anything further to say, besides the obvious. They need to communicate with someone and the fact that I am a porn star has nothing to do with it. It just means that I am more available than your usual star. Some of them were in prison but it wasn't the majority. Some people say that we would make good psychiatrists! It's probably true in a way.

The lifesaver fan. People who have risky jobs, like fire fighters, people in the military, cops. I guess porn is a great way for them to exorcize the pressure after a tough and scary day.

A lot of people other than fans wrote me, as well. I had so much anonymous hate mail. Sometimes it was hilarious! I wish I had kept them. I would have published one or two for you to have a good laugh.

Needless to say, many of them were from religious fanatics. "Burning in Hell" was a lovely quote often used (illustrated by pictures sometimes). Some people are really cute! But not every religious fanatic wrote me insults. Some wanted to save me from "it" (the BBQ feast I mean!) and were generously sending religious pamphlets with their mail.

My favorite one contained a "gardener's résumé." "Dear Rebecca Lord, I would be honored to mow your lawn…" There was another fan who wanted to be my limo driver. (All adult performers own limousines, don't you know??)

From all that junk mail, one kind keeps coming back often (and still does, but by email nowadays)—guys that send their pictures hoping to become performers. I am not against it. I understand that contacting me seems logical. But please, please, stop sending me pictures of your cock! I can assure you, it's not appealing and doesn't play in your favor, even if your ding-dong is big. It makes you look creepy! Creepier if you don't even bother sending a portrait along…

Then, there is the anonymous fan that, for about 10 years, every few months, sent me weed, taped to postcards of Seattle. It took me about six years to figure out who he was.

Funny how people assumed I smoke pot. It reminds me of that Hollywod director Matthew Bright, who called me one day from Mexico, asking me to send him weed. I only met the guy twice and we never talked about that kind of thing. Is there something about me?

In 1996, comfortably settled in our new home, one night after dinner, we were talking with Rick about Asia Carrera and how smart she is. Asia is a computer geek (among many other talents). She had told Philippe, on a set that day, that she actually just built all by herself a fan club website (Asia Carrera was the first adult performer with a website).

Rick had an epiphany: "Let's do one for Rebecca. I have no doubt— the internet is the future!!" Great idea, but how was I going to do that, exactly? I didn't know that I was sitting next to a computer geek that has been working for the government, working on radar and missiles for a few years. One day, Rick just decided to quit his job and become a photographer, which was his true passion. I couldn't be luckier. I was so excited!

Teaching Philippe and I how to create a website and how to run it took some time. Computers and software back then weren't what they are today and we had to learn everything from scratch. Our office looked like a huge Play mobile playground, computer parts were everywhere. We would go to the Reseda "swap meet" and buy parts to build a PC.

Rick came almost every day and sometimes slept over. Then, he started to sleep over more and more often. He was never in a hurry to go home.

His roommate had heavy drinking issues and when Rick was coming home at night, he sometimes had a gun pointed at him as he thought Rick was an intruder. Not sure if it was loaded or not but Rick had a couple of scares. We invited him to move in with us and become our roommate since he was in our home most of the time anyway!

Once rebeccalord.com was finally up and running, the Fan Club took on another dimension. I have to admit that being one of the two existing porn stars with a website at the time (and it remained that way for quite a while) helped tremendously in its success.

I jumped from basic offers to all kind of offers, creating various stuff. Different kinds of subscriptions, mouse pads, t-shirts, hats, playing cards, collectible cards (like baseball cards only it was me!), CD-ROMs, then DVDs (when it took over VHS), underwear, shoes, stockings… you name it. We also had the idea to offer 20 minutes custom videos, personalized. Those were striptease or/and masturbation videos that gave the fans the possibility to send their own little script. I was surprised to find out how imaginative some people could be!

But above all, I found out how many people were into fetishism in the US, which was something completely new to me.

A foot fetish video (me doing my nails or trying shoes on, or stockings, over and over for 20 minutes) was something I considered unusual, when in fact was pretty "classic." I did more foot fetish videos (with most of my clothes on) than anything I did naked.

I have to confess being glad that those early videos (especially the first 10) will never see the light of day anywhere! When a fan insisted that I mention his name regularly and that I was free to say "anything sexy" related to my action, the result was often interesting. "Hi John …blank for 3 minutes…I love painting my fingernails, it's sexy…..blank for 4 minutes…. The color is pretty, it's turning me on….blank for 3 minutes…. Oh John!"…. Blank for 5 more, and so on. I had no idea what to say.

Like I said, that was one of the "classic" ones. What follows are true collectors' items: Covering my entire body with food, playing with the food without even masturbating and faking an orgasm, takes true acting skills!!! Rubbing my navel for 20 whole minutes pretending it's my clitoris, I confirm, makes your navel red and swollen for several hours (readers, please don't try that at home!).

As for nose fetishists, yes, they do exist. Not many of them, it would be my guess, but sometimes only one can make you look at the world in a very different way...forever! I didn't have to rub it like the navel one (thank god!!) but I had to stuff my nose with honey, clean it up, then with milk, clean it again and then, finally I had to stuff it with Nutella. Neither fish nor cheese was required, which was nice.

When you're not a real professional bowler, it is rare to have your own custom bowling ball made just for you. I had one! Even more unusual is to have it "custom made" so the hole fits your big toe. I had one too!! Not only did my fan do it for me, but he also shipped it from the other side of the country. The script was extremely detailed and I even had dialogue (talking to him).

Here is the story *written by the fan*: I am playing with the bowling ball with my foot. And then, suddenly (!!), I got curious to know what the ball felt like doing the same thing but barefoot this time. At that exact moment, I must pretend that it turns me on! Standing up first, and later sitting comfortably on a sofa, I kept rubbing my foot on the bowling ball, back and forth, sideways... But this was too much of a tease, it was too cruel and I couldn't take it anymore—I had to penetrate the ball with my big toe. I did it and it felt soooooo good, I had an orgasm almost instantly!!! Time for me to take it off...but I couldn't. I tried harder, still couldn't. Half of the custom video was me trying to find a way to take that ball off of my foot! The ending is juicy: I was furious but had to give up because there was no way to get rid of it (since I tried everything). So I finally got undressed and put my nightgown on. Yes, I'm sure you figured out what I was about to do next. I went to bed with the bowling ball on, turned off the light and said, "Good night!" Surely one of the craziest moments of my "Private Custom Video" career!!

One involved plenty of clothes. I was supposed to try some clothes on and as I was dressed, each time, I was to turn into a statue/mannequin, like the kind you see in the windows of many stores, wearing clothes... very slowly, like in slow motion. I had to pretend I was fighting this horrible fate, like it was agony. Philippe was filming it, and every time I got to the point where I was talking—and then little by little I was "trying" to talk—with my face distorted and agonized, until my lips were sealed, well....he couldn't do it. You either could hear him laughing or the camera was shaking as if we were in a middle of a 6.2 earthquake. We laughed so hard that day; it took us nearly 4 hours to do it.

I am still wondering, sometimes, if one of my friends was playing tricks on me, like placing some bets to see if I was going to do it or not.

Maybe one day, when I am old and immobilized, in a hospital bed, one will dare to show up and ask me, "You remember that custom video?!"

Chapter 9

OUR FIRST HOME in L.A. was nice and cosy, located in Reseda in San Fernando Valley. We would have stayed there longer than we actually did if my neighbors' son hadn't knocked on our door, handing me pictures and magazines to sign, several times a week!

His mom and dad were usually out of town for the weekend, so their son would stay home, officially all alone and bored. In fact, he was always having friends over. Party time! Then of course, several of them would stand in front of our porch with silly smiles on their faces, a pen and a photo or a magazine in their hand. After several months of weekend parties, the "we all want to get along" neighbors' spirit had to come to an end and I stopped opening the door.

I had two boxers and they had puppies. Shortly after several refusals to open my door and sign more autographs, we received threating letters from Animal Control, accusing us of mistreating our dogs. I'm not sure it was related but we moved out pretty quickly and actually found a bigger and nicer house. A gated house, with no immediate neighbors!

We gave away all the puppies and kept two. I had a very large yard and I love dogs. I had 4 boxers at this time.

STEVE ORENSTEIN, Wicked Picture's founder, signed Jenna Jameson to an exclusive contract in 1995. Under his wing and with clever promotion, she became one of the most famous porn stars of all time.

That same year, I gave Steve one of my boxer puppies and he offered me the opportunity to shoot my first movie as a "director." He was looking for a European product and I was tempted by the experience.

I felt like I was in the adult business long enough to give it a shot. Directing a movie was a way to be creative and control what was shown the way I liked it. Plus having a female performer as a director was something uncommon at the time. As I explained earlier, it's all about marketing—it was something new and unusual.

A European product means European performers. The plan was to go to Cannes during the Hot d'Or and shoot there since many porn stars would be gathered in one place which would be cost effective. Since Nic was going there every year, we decided to share the villa together.

After only one year I was surprised to see how things had changed in France. So many new performers! Some of the people I knew had already left the Industry. I wasn't prepared for such a warm welcome.

Everyone, including the media, was all over me, like I was suddenly someone special. Many people even paid me compliments, which was odd since I was still the same person and looked identical. They didn't see me the same way they did before, only because I was making a career in the US. I was now "American" to them, and that alone was enough to get their respect. People are strange sometimes!

Nic and I had to get organized to be able to share our luxury villa. We had to figure out who shot who and when.

Sadly I didn't succeed in finishing the entire movie in Cannes. It's more complicated than it looks to shoot a movie as a director. When you're a performer and don't know any better, the only aspect you have to manage is showing up on time and doing your scene to the best of your abilities. If you can, have fun and enjoy the whole thing.

As a director, it's a whole other ballgame! You have to organize the shoot first, then make sure it all goes according to plan. Not sure I realized that it was not that simple at the time. I have to confess that the organization of this first movie was a little hectic!

I met and hired Raffaëla Anderson, Olivia Del Rio and a couple of new performers but some of them got flaky on me. I learned the hard way that I wasn't strict enough. I had a few things against me that a confirmed director didn't have to deal with. I was young. I was an adult performer, and a woman. Don't forget that the adult industry is a man's world when it comes to business.

Since I was now used to the American way, flaky people weren't something I was used to or could have expected. They don't raise talent that way in the USA! Bottom line, I had to extend my trip and finish the movie in Paris.

A female performer named Lisa Harper was part of the cast. A cute brunette, she was a newcomer that had already built a reputation for herself. She was known for being a "double anal" specialist!

Not only was it true, but she was the one asking for it when directors were booking her over the phone: "Are you sure you don't want a double-anal-penetration in your movie?"

I frankly don't get it… WHY? Why would anyone like to watch such a thing?

It is not the Cirque Du Soleil! You don't need to show someone that you can physically do extravagant things with your body. I always thought, who in his right mind would ask his girlfriend, "Hey girl, here is my friend John, do you mind if we double penetrate your butt hole tonight?"

I understand that we sell fantasy. Fine. But for me fantasy means that the viewers drool all over the superb body of a girl and how good she is at what she does. Not putting her in crazy positions that are more related to a circus than a fantasy.

What about a triple penetration, then? Anybody? It's certainly doable! As far as the girl enjoying it or not, let's just say that if you don't blink with 2 in your butt, it means you don't feel anything with one. Sad.

Aside from that, Lisa was a really nice girl. Her boyfriend on the other hand was a nightmare. The typical "pimp" some girls carry around in the porn industry. They don't work, spend the girl's money, and push them to work harder. Anyone who has flirted with the adult world has met some parasite boyfriend at least once, lazing around on a set or answering her phone.

I never understood why some actresses feels the need to be abused by guys like that, and still don't have an explanation to this day.

When *Rebecca Lord's World Tour* was finally done, I took some extra days in Paris to visit family and friends. Time had gone by and I missed them.

I was relieved to see that the ones that counted the most found a way to swallow the pill of what I did for work somehow. The other ones that were gone forever because of my job were obviously the ones that didn't count!

Seeing me safe and happy reassured them they should not worry about the bad porn star image most people have, which would be an antisocial, drug addicted nymphomaniac. As far as I'm concerned, I stopped caring about what people thought of me a long time ago. By "people" I mean people other than my loved ones.

Have you noticed that the harder you try, the less improvement you get in what people think of you? Perhaps it is simply because you just can't please everybody.

People choose to like you, or not. It comes from them, not from you. Whatever you do will never be enough and if they choose to, they will always find something they dislike in you.

Regarding the popular porn star (or unpopular, I should say, in this case) image, it works quite the same way—lots of people feel the need to believe "porn" is bad.

They need Manichaean references in their lives. *On this side it's all good, on the other side... well... must be all bad.* Apply this logic to porn. A performer has to be unhealthy and brainless, a drug addict, a sexual misfit... in one word, evil. The famous word that keeps coming back to me in lots of hate email and letters I receive regularly.

I am not making any judgments, I am just saying it's human. The more insecure you are, the safer it makes you feel to think this way. If you consider me to be a bad person for what I do then it will always make you feel better, normal, safe, integrated in society. In a word: good (as opposed to *evil*).

It's just fine the way it is. Without its so-called "negative reputation," the adult business would take a dive. "Bad" sells, and will keep selling. Did I mention that lots of those "official porn hater fanatics" are very good porn customers. Funny huh?

The media knows very well how to use the "evil porn image." On TV shows or radio, for example, they often invite the most stupid porn performer they can find. If they can't find one, they will find a way to make her look stupid. They know better than anyone what people want to hear. It makes good ratings!

The worst part in this media circus is that I even know some adult performers that will play this game on purpose in order to maintain that "bad" image.

Chapter 10

A FEW WEEKS AFTER I came back to United States, I started to receive several phone calls about a French actress, coming to L.A. for a couple of months. She needed help. Ex-colleagues, directors, productions, journalists, photographers, etc… everyone seemed to have my phone number!

Philippe and I were lucky to have someone who was there for us when we first arrived and it seemed normal to offer others that chance. It isn't easy to land into the "jungle."

The thing is, when you do a favor for somebody, it's difficult to refuse the same favor to others—you just opened a door that will be difficult to close. Believe me, it's amazing how word of mouth can fly at the speed of light sometimes, even across the ocean!

Now, the word "help" is very vague and could have various meanings. In this case, it was to arrange accommodations and guide her through the maze of adult productions, along with a few phone calls to recommend her. Many actresses came that year, and the year after. Most of them, but not all, I ran into briefly in Cannes.

My best memory was with Coralie, a French female performer. She was intelligent, fun, and charismatic with a big mouth, when she needed to have one. She was very independent and even though she stayed at our house for a while, she asked very little of us.

We didn't accommodate all of them at our place, but still, it was a frequent situation. Depending on their level of English and maturity, we often didn't have the heart to leave them all alone in big L.A. right away. Oh and last but not least—some of them didn't even have a driver's license. Not being able to drive a car in L.A. is like going to Hawaii on a kayak! Some of them even didn't have any money to rent an apartment.

Of course, it's something we usually discovered once they arrived, never before hand! As you can imagine we couldn't just dump a fellow countryman/woman the next day!

It's okay for a little while, if we all get along, but sometimes it is not that easy to manage if we don't! I have received many performers at my house. Among them Olivia Del Rio (Brazilian), Liza Harper (French) and boyfriend , Tristan Segal (French) and Angela Crystal (Czech), Bruno Sx (French), and Rumika (Romanian).

With enough time and experience, one has a tendency to think you've seen it all! Think twice, you haven't. There is nothing like doing a favor for an unknown person who turns out to be highly paranoid and won't leave your home!

"Please, she needs your help, she is fragile and she can't do it by herself. She is a close friend of mine," said the French photographer on the phone. Marine came to the US with a tiny bag and a large smile on her face. I met her at a convention in Vegas; she was going to conquer Hollywood. "Be ready people—here I am!!!"

We realized almost instantly that she was different. A little "gone," if you know what I mean. She wasn't a bad person at all. She was just lost and living in her own fantasy world, in her head, very far away in another galaxy!

This was one of the reasons why we took her home. Her instability, and vulnerability, was too obvious and she would have become the perfect target for unscrupulous people.

One of the things Philippe and I have in common is that when we accept something we usually assume the responsibility for it no matter what the consequences. Which took us too far sometimes.

First there was an incident at the hotel in Vegas. She sat in the corridor in a sofa not far from my room on the same floor. Of course I didn't know. I heard knocking at my door at 2 a.m. and when I opened the door, a guy from hotel security asked me if I knew her and explained she couldn't sleep on the sofa. I should have known then that things were not going to go well.

Marine expected everything to be done for her. Whatever help we gave her or whatever we did was simply not enough. She was acting like we were on her payroll! She even yelled at us sometimes for not getting results quickly enough!!! We had to patiently explain to her that we had our lives and our world didn't revolve around her all the time.

The worst part for me was her following me…everywhere! I am not kidding. She was all over me all the time. She would never give me a break even in my own house.

Let me put it this way. If I was in the kitchen, so was Marine. If I was leaving the kitchen for the living room, Marine was already passing in front of me like the Wile Coyote cartoon character, to be one step ahead of me in the living room!

Once I went to the restroom for some "alone time." She went there too and sat on the floor. She really did! Nothing was stopping her!

We would have sex in our bedroom, door closed of course, and she would enter the room and sit, looking at us and declare, "Don't worry about me, go ahead, I've seen it many times." We were so astonished that we couldn't find any reply!

I surprised myself by hiding once or twice in my own house, saying out loud, "I am going to the BBQ outside," pretending I was going in the yard but running to another room and locking myself in, still holding sausages and T-Bones on a plate. You should have seen the look on her face when I came out finally. She looked like a sulking five year old.

I must confess that Marine could be obnoxious but also hilarious. At the time, there were no cell phones yet, or they were extremely expensive. But we did have pagers.

If you never had a pager, the concept was to leave your phone number manually, like a text message, so the person you want to reach can call you back. We used it a LOT for work.

After introducing Marine to everyone, I was surprised that she didn't get work. Two weeks had gone by and no one was calling her back. Which was weird since Marine was pretty and pleasant, at first sight at least!

Suspicious and paranoid, she blamed it on me, of course—I must have done something wrong.

Then one day, we understood why. Philippe and I witnessed her contacting productions and we almost choked with laughter. Marine was leaving voice messages for everyone, on their pagers.

Two weeks are enough for productions to forget faces, they see so many, and the only way to remind people she was still around was to bring her with me on a set. While I was working, it would give her another opportunity to see them and it would be faster. Bad mistake!

I took her with me on the set of *Strap-on Sally*, a series starring Chantilly Lace. I knew the production manager very well and he suggested she could be in the giant, all girls orgy scene. The more the merrier. I translated to the make-up artist her preferences about make-up, helped her chose her strap-on, and introduced her to the other performers. I explained to her what the director wanted and he was very specific that the orgy would be everywhere in the living room, in the stairway and the balcony above the living room. He wanted to do a one-shot sequence, no cut. Marine said she understood, no worries.

The director yelled "action" and the cameraman began shooting. All the girls started going at it with strap-ons, dildos and whatnot, the cameraman among them doing his one-shot sequence. Then suddenly I heard coming from the upper balcony, "Rebecca, have you seen my hair brush?"

The director looked at me furiously and I wished I could have hidden in one of those small mouse holes! Of course, we had to redo the whole thing and of course, she always found something to ask me from her balcony while we were shooting. She couldn't find her lipstick, then she wanted my car keys to get something. No matter what I said, no matter what the director yelled at her, she would invariably talk to me from the balcony. The director gave up after a few tries and he decided to cut her interventions at the editing.

I also took her to San Diego with me on another set. Since the past had taught me something, I asked her gently to try and listen to what people asked of her.

Marine in one of her paranoid moods, meaning every time I talked to someone in English, she thought I was talking about her. She also acted like she was doing a break up scene with me in front of everybody. The entire crew was starting to look at me in a strange way. Believe me, in those kinds of situations, even if you don't speak the same language, people can feel exactly what you are saying!

This time I was in the middle of my scene and she just walked into the room and interrupted my sex scene to ask for my blow dryer! Another time she opened the door in tears, looked at me, said something I couldn't understand in French, and closed it. I thought something bad had happened, so I asked for a 5-minute break and went to see her in the make-up room.

She explained that nobody liked her, nobody was paying attention to her and she wanted to go home. I was very upset and explained to her that she couldn't go into the room and talk to me during my scene. She said she had "whispered!" Well let me tell you the crew and I agreed that she must have learned how to whisper inside a helicopter surrounded by fucking chainsaws! She got pissed off at me for not understanding her and laughing about the "whisper" thing, so she declared that she wanted a back to L.A.

I finished my scene, making sure she would not interrupt again, and we drove back to L.A. It didn't go very well. I was upset.

I am not proud to tell you that I kicked her out of my car and left her on the side of the freeway. My wish at that point was to find a way to get rid of her permanently and since I couldn't physically strangle her, this was the best compromise I could find. I remember vividly the feeling of freedom while the car was going away, watching her getting smaller and smaller in the rear view mirror.

Unfortunately, that awesome feeling only lasted several seconds since I went back to get her. Fortunately, she felt she couldn't stay any longer with monsters like us, so she flew back to France, shortly after this event occurred.

I have told friends that story many times and they all look at me with consternation. What a weird world you live in, Rebecca!

Probably. But looking at all this several years later makes me smile. In a way, Marine was animating my life, preparing me for what would come next. She was making me stronger and smarter when it comes to relationships with adult performers.

Today I produce and direct movies and deal with a lot of talent. They are all very different, some in a good way, some in a not so good way.

To give you an idea how popular we were for having people over and helping them, Philippe got hired by Vivid, an adult company, as an official translator, on sets, when needed. As for me, I got pressured to start my own international agency for foreign performers, which I refused, for the reason I shared with you earlier about agents. Putting aside the heavy responsibilities, babysitting wasn't exactly what I call "dream work!"

Sometimes you're also too late when it comes to help people. Among the French female performers I tried to help was Chanonne. She landed in the US with a different plan than most. Her goal was to stay and build a career in L.A.

She was mature enough to get her own place and find work. I hired her for a movie I directed for Sin City and we got along very well. We even used to go out together, from time to time. It looked like everything was going according to plan for her.

Until one day, I got a message from her on my answering machine: "Hi guys, I need your help, please, it's extremely urgent that you call me back." She said this in French and then, "My number is: xxxxxxxxx," in English!

Her accent was horrible and she spoke in a hurry, half stammering! It was impossible to understand the number.

We tried every combination of numbers and nothing worked. We were never able to get hold of her! We waited, anxiously, for Chanonne to call us back, but she never did.

A couple of weeks later, we heard from the magazine *Hot Video* that her parents, having heard no news, were looking for her persistently. The girl had simply vanished. No one could find her. I hated myself for a very long time for not being able to understand the number. Many years later, I saw a picture of her on the Internet. She looked completely different but it was her. There were tears in my eyes, I was really relieved. Chanonne was alive!

She was doing some live shows and I was able to ask her how she was doing. She said she was okay, but nothing more. Obviously she didn't want to talk about the day that she called. Who knows what happened during all that time. I have a bad feeling that it wasn't anything good.

Imagine dealing with a situation like this one on a daily basis. Becoming an agent? Me? No way! I want to stay sane for as long as I can!

We moved quite a lot during our time in L.A. Sometimes by choice, sometimes by necessity. It didn't bother us that much, actually. Moving into a new home felt almost like a new start each time. Renting places gives you that kind of freedom. My friend Rick stayed with us for years and every time I announced to him that I was looking for a new place, he shook his head, in an amazed kind of way, like he expected it.

Many "civilians" have asked me what was I saying to Real Estate agencies or landlords about my job. With experience, I got good at it, but the first few times were awkward. Since I could be a terrible liar, I decided to disguise the truth instead. My answer to them was that I worked in the entertainment industry. If anyone was curious enough to insist, I would say in a blurry way, "Many various aspects, I don't have a specialty." It usually discouraged people and left them without any further questions since I was so vague about it.

In some situations, like during a dinner party for example, when I met friends of a friend, I'd try a more risky approach, depending on the feeling I had with the person I spoke with. I tested their reaction with a quick, "I am in the erotic entertainment business."

If their pupils suddenly got dilated or if they had a hard time swallowing their glass of Chardonnay, I'd pull back right away explaining I kind of exaggerated. It was mostly "lingerie stuff!" In 20 years I managed to go on telling the tale and always made sure that other women at the table wouldn't freak out and ask their husbands or boyfriends to leave the party immediately!

Am I ashamed of what I do for a living? Absolutely not. I only worked that hard at my statements for two reasons. First, it is a form of respect to the friend that we have in common. I don't want to ruin his reputation or embarrass him in front of everybody.

Second, it is pure laziness! If by any chance the person is open minded enough not to be freaked by the kind of work I do, my evening is over.

Being in the adult world arises the curiosity of most people and they always have a billion questions to ask. The funniest thing is that they often don't want to know the truth. They want me to say what they expected or turn them on. They probably imagine that it's a permanent orgy to be part of the adult industry!

The truth is that it is not very sexy once it is explained to civilians—long hours on the set, technical problems, the permanent "stop and go" during the scenes. It's usually frustrating for them to hear the naked truth about porn. Our work is difficult to explain. You have to live it to understand it. Sometimes I tell them stories, sexy ones, or funny ones, because I can see in their eyes that it's totally not what they expected.

Anyway, if they love hearing the stories, it's no more fun for me that evening! I'll get stuck with the person for hours. Next time I'll stick to the "erotic entertainment job!"

The most interesting part is when you are somewhere and no one asks you what you do for a living. It is a strange feeling. You shake hands, introduce yourself, get into conversations, laugh, eat, drink, then, here comes nothing! No one asks what your job is.

Then you ask people what they do, hear them talk about themselves for a while and still nothing. By then, of course, I figured it out. It used to make me uncomfortable, thinking they all knew me before I even knew them, but now I'm amused by it.

I discreetly look at them one by one and watch if THEY are uncomfortable with me around. It's fun! You probably wonder how I manage to make friends with civilians, then. Well it isn't easy. I even have to admit, it is pretty rare. My only option is to let the person I like get to know me first. Then, slowly, I bring the truth to the table. I've surprised a few that way!

I tricked a few landlords into renting me their places not knowing what I do for a living, but I got tricked as well! At one point, we rented a huge, gorgeous, three level designer house. We had the idea to rent it, once in a while, as a location for adult productions. That didn't last. I couldn't stand having people going through my personal stuff. One or two days' rental meant rent paid for the month!

Since it was such a luxury place and I wanted it so badly, I was more careful than usual during our meetings with the landlords. I dressed really conservatively and tried to chat like I was having a 5 p.m. tea conversation! The old couple seemed very nice and we were thrilled when we signed the lease.

For that year we were extra careful not to let anything show. We ended up hiding fan club products or anything related to porn in a room and locked it. Then, for my birthday, we threw a big party. The kind of party where people get so drunk they cannot drive back home! (It didn't help that one of my boxers stole and ate the main course in the kitchen while we were having the appetizers!) So most of my guess slept wherever they could. Meaning people were passed out everywhere in my house. Bedrooms, living room, the den...

Guess who decided to stop by, unexpectedly, the next morning around 8 a.m.? I panicked, ran like hell, picking up clothes on the floor, waking everybody up so they could hide downstairs, begging them to hurry.

Somehow I even managed to hide all the empty bottles in a few seconds. I then opened the door like nothing happened and the landlady nicely gave me one of the shutter remote controls that was missing. How wonderful.

As I shut the front door, I turned around and had a glimpse of my face in the mirror on the wall. I then realized what I looked like that morning. My eye shadow from the night before was down to my cheeks and my eyeliner seemed to have had way too much fun running around all over my face. Another tiny detail—my blouse was wide open and the pants I was wearing weren't mine.

I really got upset over this. Which made the old couple burst out laughing, a year later, as we were moving out, when they revealed to me they knew all along about our jobs. Their son was an adult performer himself. Talk about improbability! I had a hollow laugh.

The landlord that followed was an ordinary family man. A psychiatrist, if I remember well. Judging by his appearance and the way he talked, he seemed to be a conservative person.

It was such an embarrassment the day he came over to look at a leak from my bathroom to my bedroom! Looking at my bedroom's hardwood floor to seek any damage it might have caused, he bent over to look closer under my bed and then suddenly he said, "What is this?" What followed was even more unexpected. "Oh my gosh, you have a dildo in there!"

Oooops. I was red as a tomato and confused. I dived under the bed, hoping it would buy me some time to find an explanation.

What a nightmare. Without a flashlight I couldn't see anything, it was too dark. I kept asking, "Where, where?" I stayed underneath there, searching, way too long to seem normal and sane. I had to get up at some point, and face him.

When I finally did, he looked at me, smiled, and said, "I was just kidding!" I could have ripped his eyes out! I didn't know what to say. My surprise was such that I could hardly react to the creepy joke! He seemed really amused.

A couple of months later, he came back, seriously preoccupied by something. Our gardener had called him, saying we were growing marijuana in our basement. The only thing he asked from us was to show him the basement to prove him wrong.

Which is very easy to do when you don't have the room full of sex toys, adult magazines and hundreds of tapes/ DVDs with me on the cover! When I say full, I really mean it. You couldn't walk in! It was all the stuff I needed for my fan club and going on the road. So of course I had to refuse. Imagine the misunderstanding that it created. No matter what I could say or any pretexts I could make up, it wouldn't change the fact that he thought I had been caught. I didn't want a "war" between tenant and landlord. But I couldn't show him the basement full of porn stuff.

I guess he finally believed me. But then we were worried and half paranoid for a while until he showed up again, on a Halloween afternoon dressed as Howard Stern.

When I complimented him about his costume, his answer was how much he loved the show and that he was a huge fan of Howard Stern. Then he blinked! It occurred to me that I had been invited on the show twice already!

That's when I realized that my landlord was playing with me! He had known who I was for a while.

Looking back, I think that guy was pretty funny. He certainly got a kick out of this.

For the record, if I think some people might judge me because of what I do, I surely should be totally unprejudiced towards them. It works both ways. The ditch is pretty large between the civilian and the adult world and sometimes, trying to give a positive image of yourself makes you forget that you should try not to judge others by what they appear to be.

Chapter 11

PART OF MY JOB included doing promotions. It could be movie promotions, or a new sex shop's grand opening, but also TV network promotions like Playboy or Spice Channel. It consisted of going places all over the US and it usually required three to four days of travel. Spice Channel was doing a lot of promotions and they hired me very often for several years. The fun part is that you never knew where you were going to wind up. From big cities to small towns in the middle of nowhere, I loved discovering the US. Every place is unique and the people from one state to another aren't the same. Depending on where you go, it even seems like a different country sometimes.

Between my work and driving across the country yearly, on a road trip with my husband, I am very pleased to have visited all 50 states. I can't get enough of it, its scenery, and its complexity. I am just in love with the variety of what the US has to offer.

Representing an erotic network has its pluses, compared to an adult company—the access to the public is less limited. Unlike the adult companies, which involve lots of restrictions, we could promote the channel in almost any place, such as sport events, festivals, and nightclubs. I found it refreshing!

My planning was simple and easy. We'd arrive one day before the "signings." I'd advertise our presence on a local radio station to come see us, to bring as many people as possible. This exercise has been really beneficial to me. It got very useful when the time came to do my own promotions. Unexpectedly, I sometimes also made the trip, only to escort someone from the TV station to a dinner with clients. This could have been boring depending on who the dinner party was, but luckily I was often escorting the same girl. Her name was April. She was a sweet little Mexican girl, around 5 feet tall. She was always exited to get out of the office for some travel that included sophisticated meals and drinks. Somehow she often managed to be the one selected to go! April and I got along very well and the couple of days we were spending together somewhere felt more like a girl trip than work.

Back in the '90s, full movies were still being shot. Little by little, adult films with two versions mostly replaced them, one hardcore and one softcore. It's really not the same. I am happy to have had the chance to participate in several real erotic movies, not the softcore version of a hardcore film.

I like erotic movies. I find them sophisticated and sexy for the most part. I had the chance to work with a director I always admired: Andrew Blake. It was before he created his own company (Studio A) and began to shoot a few adult films as well. I just love Andrew Blake's style.

When Philippe interviewed him for a magazine, we discovered that Andrew even won an award for Best Art Director at an international film festival. Somehow I wasn't surprised. He also worked with Helmutt Newton, of whom I am a big fan. What I think makes Andrew Blake special, beside his skills, which are obvious, is his feeling towards women. You can see he admires them by the way he brings them out, magnifies them. He shoots brunettes, blondes, skinny or voluptuous girls, it doesn't matter.

What is important is the sensuality he finds in each of them. The first time I worked for him, was in New York City in 1995. It was also my first time there. I didn't have time to see much of the city and it was very frustrating. I felt attracted to it like nowhere else. I had to come back! What I didn't know yet was that NYC was going to be my number one destination for my dancing performances in strip clubs a couple of years later.

In my opinion, only a few porn directors are that talented. I believe Cameron Grant, Michael Ninn and Greg Dark belong to the same category. Even though they all have different styles, they have one thing in common: they all have a diploma from art school.

Gregory Dark, for example, had an MFA. He is known in the adult industry for his eccentricity. His movies are just weird. He liked to put strange clowns on the screen, or voyeur dwarfs to give a perverted aspect to his movies. He enjoyed having the performers disguised in an eccentric way. He was unique that way. He didn't care if people liked his movies or not, his only motivation was to shoot whatever he decided he would be shooting. He had a little book where he wrote every dream he could remember, then would bring it to the screen with all its craziness.

Greg was already a director in Hollywood, under a different name of course, and for a while, he tried to be in two different worlds at the same time. He was just having fun! That guy was the craziest and at the same time one of the nicest people I have ever known.

He explained to me that all he was trying to do was to put his own fantasies on screen. If you knew him, you would understand how frustrated he must have been—most of his fantasies were too insane to be seen anywhere!

Once, he insisted on shooting a scene with Roxanne Hall, in a bathtub full of worms. Roxanne nearly died laughing. "Only for a quick masturbation scene!" he said. I don't know if he ever succeeded in finding someone who would do it, but the scene surely never got released!

Let me add one more, I insist. I personally provided full satisfaction for him for this one. It involved a chocolate cake. To be more specific, Greg's dream was to have somebody cook a chocolate cake for him. That's it!

He didn't want to have dinner, then a cake for desert, or go to a restaurant or even have a chocolate cake bought for him. All he cared about was to have me cooking one.

His fantasy had important details—I needed to send him an official invitation by mail, and to have him over at my house. I tried to explain that my cooking performance is known to be a disaster but it only made it worse. The less I knew how cook, the more excited he was. Part of me thought it was a joke, so I accepted the bet and followed his rules, out of curiosity.

Surprisingly enough, Greg was blown away by my gesture. He kept repeating how happy he was and that no one had ever done this for him. He ate his cake like it was the best thing he ever put in his mouth. My cake recipe was from a children's book. I watched him, speechless. I was only too happy to have helped.

In 2000, Gregory Dark left the adult industry because his success was starting to be in his work with traditional films. It's too difficult to combine both because of the negative reputation that comes with working in porn. He called me one night to tell me how boring his wealthy new life was. How can someone be bored shooting video clips, TV series and movies, when most people would kill to have his dream job?? Well, again, that's Greg.

In my line of work, becoming a feature dancer in the US is quite common. Unlike many of my female colleagues, who sometimes became a porn star after a couple of movies, only so they could feature dance afterwards, it wasn't something I was attracted to do. But I decided to give it a try and see if I liked it. Who knows, maybe it would be fun.

I got an offer from a strip club in Philadelphia and I signed a contract for 21 shows in 6 days. My only condition was that my friend Rick had to come with me. First, I needed a bodyguard. Second, my friend was familiar with the system. He had been roadie several times before, for other porn stars.

It was exciting preparing the shows. Choosing what kind of music to play, what kind of props to use to play with towards the end of each show to make some kind of interaction with the crowd. Like a gun full of milk to hand out to people, to shoot at me wherever they liked. Candles that don't burn your skin to pour on my body, and so on.

Of course, there were costumes, too. I was a biker bitch, a nurse, a G-I Jane, a cheerleader and a classy pin-up from the '30s

When we arrived in Philly, it was a little disappointing to find out the club and our hotel wasn't in the city itself, but in the suburbs. But it was nothing compared to my first step into the club. It didn't look at all like "Bob's Classy Lady," a strip club I had visited in L.A. before to make my decision. The club was dark, filthy looking, and there was only one customer sitting in a corner of the stage. I couldn't see if he was sleeping or not.

Worse was what was on stage. One stripper stood alone, naked on stage, dragging her feet, like she was imitating some zombie movements.

My dressing room, behind the stage, was very large and empty. There was a huge mirror on one side, surrounded by a dark green carpet on each wall. My guess is that they decorated it sometime around 1970.

The walls were covered with Porn Star's graffiti. It read: "I was here," "hang in there," "I survived, it's your turn"... like in jail! Six days? I wanted to scream!

The next day, my show started at 11 a.m. We showed up armed with cockroach spray, just in case. We were at the club one hour before it opened to have enough time to get ready. The club was still empty. Rick was doing his best to reassure me, saying the club advertised the show times and it was logical that nobody was there yet.

As I was getting ready, I could hear from my dressing room anything that was going on outside my door. Its emptiness made any sound reverberate and the music wasn't enough to cover it. I heard my only two customers arriving a few seconds before I was up.

They were shouting and banging the runway's edge. They seemed very drunk. Stripping in public for the first time is enough to make you nervous. But this? I was overcome with fear! The whole thing was just too gloomy.

It was too late to run, the D.J was making the announcement. The Biker Bitch stormed the door and made her first appearance!

That said, I didn't follow any advice Rick gave me, of course, and instead of taking my clothes off very slowly and gradually to make it last as long as possible, I was on stage 17 minutes which is a long time to stare at the wall. I was butt naked before the end of my first song, with three more to go!

Even worse, to give style to my striptease, I decided somehow to throw every piece of my costume in every dark corner of the club. Now what? I just blew any chance to appear busy. No pole dance to make cute little turns with! Nothing! Just a wide long slippery runaway and the stage. Fifteen minutes to go. Someone please make me magically disappear!

My lovely drunk customers, who were a dad and his son apparently, were now banging their feet on the floor. The sound system was so low, it never covered their noises.

The only thing left to do was to be a puppet. So I smiled and walked back with force. I walked again and again, until one of them did the unthinkable. He threw a banana at me! I tried to remain calm, but seriously?

I understood later on the purpose of the banana. They thought I forgot my sex toys and they were trying to be helpful. People's generosity and sacrifice blow me away sometimes!

The music finally stopped. It was over. I picked up my only dollar bill on the floor and thanked everyone by waving at the crowd, like a rock star in front of thousand people.

I never felt more humiliated. This experience was so degrading to me! Even if the club was paying me to be there, unlike house girls that make their living with tips, I was under the impression that I showed my body and made a fool of myself for one dollar! Twenty shows left to do seemed like an inferno.

I was a newcomer in the US and wasn't sure what the consequences would be if I left the club and breached my contract. Depressed, I was going to stay until the end.

Happily I had Rick with me. He did everything he could to keep my spirits up, every minute of every day. He even called a friend of his, who was in town for a few days, to throw dollar bills on stage during my shows, to motivate the others around him. His friend Alvin was the kind of guy who you don't have to repeat twice what to do. That guy was pouring money like a maniac! The biggest crowd I had was seven people, including Alvin, on a Saturday night. Before each show, I was as petrified as if it were the first time. Strange thing, as everyone says the fear passes as it goes on. It didn't work at all for me!

There were some slight changes on stage, though. I stopped right away being naked after two minutes. It was quite the opposite. I kept my clothes on as long as I could. I didn't want to take them off anymore!

I remember refusing alcohol before my show. The truth is, I was really tempted, but I figured that if I would drink once and it helped, I was going to do it before each performance. I have compassion for the girls that fell into that trap. Life is testing you sometimes.

Anyway, after such a horrible experience, I made a promise to never "go on the road" again. My dancing career was over. It was interesting to find out, shortly after, that having an agent that specialized in booking adult film stars in clubs was kind of mandatory!

There are too many clubs in the US to be able to select from them. To give you a vague idea, a state like Minnesota had more than 40 strip clubs at the time, so imagine how may there are in the rest of country.

The tricky part isn't always their standards—it's mainly what law the clubs depend on. It varies all the time! The state law, the county law, the city, all are different! It's enough to be completely lost. For example, full nudity could be legal in some states but not in a certain county or city.

You could be in a town were having contact with customers is illegal, by this I mean touching the stripper during lap dances or when a dancer sits on people's laps, and 40 miles further, it's legal! Overall, I learned that clubs who serve alcohol are usually only topless, as opposed to nude clubs with soft drinks only. As for having contact with customers, the nude ones prohibit it. But there are too many exceptions. Add to that, the official law and the unofficial rules, and my head was spinning! Dancing was not for me.

Chapter 12

I HAD BEEN CONTACTED unexpectedly by someone through my website. His name was Greg Mielcarz and he presented himself as being with public relations at Planet Hollywood. You may ask yourself, "Why?" I did, too.

I thought he was either a fake or he had "something" in mind. Of course, the best way to find out was to accept his lunch invitation and see what came out of it.

I wasn't too comfortable during our meeting. I was rather paranoid and I couldn't figure out the reason he contacted me. Especially when Greg announced that I could come to dinner often, at the restaurant on Hollywood Boulevard for free, and with whomever I wanted to bring along. I was skeptical. What was the catch? People don't feed strangers for free, except in some non-profit International Food Association, let alone at Planet Hollywood!

Once again, if you don't try, you'll never know! So I went, with my husband.

Greg nicely took the time to give us the big tour and we visited the private rooms for movie's opening nights and private showings. We had a lovely dinner and that was it! I was welcome back anytime.

Needless to say, I took him up on his offer and went back with friends, then family, many times after. Like I mentioned before, my cooking skills weren't one of my best virtues and we were going out for dinner all the time anyway!

With time, Greg and I became friends. We both liked to ride horses and we enjoyed riding together in the Sunland area, where the land offers many parks for miles without construction.

I was also invited to movies' opening nights, like *Six Days, Seven Nights* with Harrison Ford and Anne Heche, and parties, like one for Demi Moore's birthday.

I could be wrong, but I like to think Greg approached me at first because his point of view was different from most people. As a public relations guy, maybe he thought having me around sometimes was a plus, some kind of a discreet provocation perhaps? It isn't usually how people think and it takes a very open mind to have thought of it.

It is probably why he wanted us to meet before inviting me often—to see if I was decent and presentable. Anyway, Greg is now the head of marketing for Morgan Creek. I am so proud of him! He is one of the great guys.

One company I often worked for, as talent, was Sin City Entertainment. The general manager of the company, Hank, happened to like the movie I directed and offered me a bigger budget to make one for them, but this time, in the US. We ended up agreeing for two movies, back to back. We called them *Sensation 1 & 2*.

Directing those two movies was a challenge, a very big one. It was just one disaster after another. To start with, I still had difficulties with some performers who had a hard time picturing me as a director.

In 1996, being both a director and a performer was unusual, especially for a girl. I understood their lack of adaptability. I really did, but what a pity that I had to fight constantly on the set. That wasn't my only problem, though.

I should have known things were going to be difficult after the first day. The owner of the place I was renting vanished after we walked in, and locked the gate by mistake. Technically it shouldn't have stopped us from shooting inside, except the truck with the equipment wasn't there yet and neither were all the performers. So most of the cast and crew couldn't get in. Needless to say, the guy was unreachable! This is how I lost the budget on day number one.

It didn't get any better. The next morning, my cameraman called me from the hospital. He was attacked by his own pit bull. The dog almost tore his arm apart! Picture a one-armed cameraman! My production problem was nothing compared to his, but anyway, it's how I lost part of the budget for day number two. I finally managed to shoot after I replaced him with another cameraman called Barry Wood, a very friendly and talented English guy. His accent was very heavy and I always thought it was worse than mine, but people confirmed I was wrong. I shouldn't have asked.

I wanted a night scene but I did not want to use artificial light for once. I wanted to use candles instead. There were hundreds of candles everywhere around the performers. As beautiful as it would have been, we had to light them first.

It became such a surprise to see the first burning candles already melted as we were trying to light the last ones! It took hours and several crewmembers to make it work. Another tiny detail escaped me as well—

the small room was deprived of oxygen and we had difficulties breathing. One by one, we had to leave the room every ten minutes, to breathe, and come back in. This went on for hours. Between overtime, double time and two days of equipment, locations, crewmembers and talent paid for nothing, my budget exploded. I was way over budget and I ended up paying from my own pocket, and I worked for free.

Once finished and fully edited, no one could tell what we went through. The movies actually looked great and turned out to sell very well! They even got nominated several times for some awards and *Sensation 1* made the "Top 100 X-rated movies of all time." How unexpected!

This particular experience taught me that I was on the wrong side of the business. I did all the work and didn't get any financial compensation out of it. From now on, I was going to produce the movies I directed, then sell them to who might be interested.

It was obvious to me at this point that a good movie requires good editing. I was lucky to have found two great guys that I kept using, faithfully, many years after.

Kenny and James Di Giorgio were two associates in San Fernando Valley, with great editing systems. They were officially working on mainstream movies and TV series. Being workaholics, they were tempted to accept job offers from the adult industry as well. Which was complicated since, as I mentioned before, you can easily ruin your reputation by mixing both.

Their solution was to organize a schedule: adult movies were to be edited at night and mainstream stuff during the day. A director must sit down with his editor, from time to time, to explain what his vision of the movie is. But I found myself staying every night, watching them work. I was fascinated by what could be done! Those guys were magicians to me.

Philippe joined us as well through curiosity and became even more passionate about it than I was! He was more intrigued by the technical part of it and I by the aestheticism of the picture. In love with their job, Kenny and James were happy to show us many things. By the year 2000, they taught us enough, so we were able to edit on our own.

Sin City Entertainment replaced their general manager shortly after my movies were made. Mickey Blank wanted to make changes in the company, like for example, hiring exclusive contract girls.

Only a few adult companies work that way. The concept is to hire a girl on a monthly payroll, with a year contract minimum, and promote the hell out of her. The more famous she becomes, the more movies she will sell. Most of the girls want to become "exclusive," since they work way less as a performer, for the same or better monthly financial compensation. It's a win-win situation.

Years later, it is also a major advantage for their dancing gigs, since they can raise their rates and improve conditions tremendously.

Mickey offered me that opportunity, along with two other girls, Kaitleen Ashley and Kylie Ireland, and I accepted it. It is common that an exclusive talent doesn't have to work every month. Sometimes we would spend weeks sitting around before shooting a movie. That's exactly what happened to us the first month, after we signed the contract.

A second month passed and it became strange not to have any news, especially when no one was answering our phone calls anymore. I showed up at the office to ask what was going on and I ran into the new general manager who was just settling in. Mickey was gone.

He apologized but explained that he wasn't going to follow Mr. Blank's decision on having contract girls. I remember thinking, "What are we? Puppets?" I felt betrayed and insulted.

His apologies weren't enough! I called Kaitleen and Kylie in a heartbeat and asked them to fight this with me. I was going to contact a lawyer and see what could be done about the situation. The contract we had was legit. Too afraid of the negative consequences that could affect their career, the other two girls decided not to follow suit.

Their reaction wasn't too surprising. Imagine a young girl facing a huge adult production company. It is intimidating. They thought that pissing them off could end their career. The thing is, and this was exactly my point: the company knew the weight of their power and they were taking advantage of the situation.

My lawyer was absolutely certain that this kind of breach of contract (i.e. for no valuable reason) gave me total rights in court. I then decided to sue them. In fact, also sad but true, a young female (victim) against a big adult company (monsters) that abused her, the court would have just too much fun condemning them. They could have hired the best lawyer there is, but they wouldn't have stood a chance.

Two hours before appearing in court, I received a phone call from Sin City's attorney. They wanted to avoid going to court and were offering a settlement. They made me a "worth-my-while" offer and everyone put that "misunderstanding" behind them.

It never affected my career. Giving me bad publicity would have been only giving them bad publicity as well. It was better for them to keep that story hidden from the media.

Chapter 13

MOMO, THE JAPANESE PHOTOGRAPHER I wrote about earlier, contacted me from Japan to share a project he had in mind. His goal was to fly me there, to Tokyo. Adult video productions and magazines would become associates for the occasion, to make the trip worthwhile for me.

Before he made it happen, he wanted to know if I was up for it. Was he kidding? Japan? I was thrilled! I was jumping up and down and said yes without any hesitation.

Meanwhile, I looked for a reference, someone who I could talk to, who had been there already, and had similar experience in Japan. It was a complete surprise to find out that no other adult actress had gone there to work. Only one, in the '80s. Tracy Lords. But needless to say, she was out of reach!

When the time came to finalize the plan, everything was square and straightforward. I was going there for a few weeks to shoot two movies, layouts for a few magazines like *Dick* magazine, and there would be lots of promotion and interviews, and dancing in various clubs. Ouch, the last one caused a psychological problem for me, as you might imagine!

The only reason I finally accepted was because dancing there had nothing to do with what I did in Philly. The approach was completely different—one show per club, with the guarantee of a certain amount of people, by contract, in clubs that aren't strip clubs, but nightclubs! The financial compensation was also quite reassuring.

As for Momo, his job was to be my personal guide during my entire time in Japan and he was hired to be my translator as well. I trusted him well enough to be comforted by his presence with me the whole time there. I was so excited, I couldn't wait!

The arrival in Japan was a real culture shock. I lost my bearings rather quickly and was quite overwhelmed. To start with, people bend over to salute you, some even several times in a row. Not knowing the meaning between one time and several, I just copied what they were doing. It took me a while to realize that the more I bowed, the more they kept doing it. It was ridiculous.

Their welcome was absolutely amazing. So many people were there! Everyone I bowed to had a gift for me. Kimonos, Japanese dolls, flowers, any gift that would represent Japan, they thought of it. I was spoiled. They made me feel like a princess or a famous rock star. I'm not sure which. To be honest, it was disproportionate to my celebrity status, but it felt great!

I was then given a large envelope. It was the detailed planning of my trip in Tokyo. I couldn't believe it. Every single little thing was scheduled, prepared and organized for me. Starting from the minute I'd wake up until it was time to go to bed. Wake up time 7 a.m., shower 7:10 a.m., room service 7:30 a.m., meeting with the crew in the lobby 8 a.m., limo 8:20 a.m., make up: 8:50 a.m., and so on until bedtime!

What if I wanted my room service before taking a shower? I guess I was out of luck. The positive part was that I couldn't be lost between my bed and the shower since they were only 5 feet apart from each other. With that tremendous gain of time, I even think I should have suggested them to put my shower time at 8:07 a.m.

Don't get me wrong, the hotel was fantastic, it's just that everything in Japan is so tiny! Apartments and hotel rooms look like dollhouses. If you get there with large US luggage, well, it's either you or your luggage that gets in!

Physically speaking, Tokyo, to me, is the exact opposite of Los Angeles. No Cobb salad syndrome there, that's for sure!

Anyway, I took the time to read my precise schedule and something else struck me. Even my meals, lunch and dinner, were planned as business meetings. I was going to meet new people during those times and the purpose of it was only to meet them! A price was next to each meal and depending upon whom I was meeting, the price changed. I was getting paid for it! Talk about unusual! It was the same principal with a few offices visits, during the day. I would be introduced to producers or magazine's owners that weren't part of the project. Visiting monuments and some of Tokyo's areas were scheduled for picture promotion. I was glad to be able to see a little bit of the city.

The next morning, in the lobby, Momo introduced me to Yuka. She was his mistress. As a married man, he had an official mistress that everyone knew about, including his wife. In fact I heard his wife and mistress were friends. Knowing I wasn't too familiar with that kind of situation, Momo explained that it wasn't unusual in Japanese culture to have both.

Yuka was appointed to be my personal assistant in case I needed anything. She was going to follow me everywhere, day and night. Her devotion was impressive and left me a little uncomfortable at times.

This was her first gig as an assistant, since she had a permanent and successful job as a fashion designer, but she seemed to have done it all her life. Yuka was lovable and she was just the sweetest girl I have ever met.

The movie's story line was to film Rebecca LOAD (yes, I was Rebecca Load, there! Ahaha) discovering Japanese culture. From holding chopsticks during a meal, to learning how to write my name in Japanese, all the way to being exposed to their sexual habits. I was to enjoy learning their "secrets."

The most memorable discovery I made was one of their sexual habits. They brought me to a special building, where in each apartment a girl was waiting for her clients. The fact that this procedure was fully legal wasn't what surprised me. What did was what was happening inside those walls.

Each place had themes—clients were going in with very precise requests. For example, building "A" was a place specialized for fingering people's butt. Building "B," for fellatio, building "C" for masturbation, and so on. Clients were very respectful of the rules and there was never any uncontrolled behavior. The apartment was extremely clean, and everything was white: the walls, the floor, and furniture. It almost looked like a clinic.

When the client arrived, he would immediately take his shoes off and then, right after, he would directly go to the bathroom to wait for the woman. She would join him and prepare the shower. Both would go in and she would wash him to make sure it is properly done.

Only then, both would go to the main room and start doing whatever was on the "menu." The rule was not to ask for more or anything other than what the place offered. I'm guessing that if a guy wanted anything else, he had to go somewhere else!

In my schedule, I had to go to a club, as a customer this time. It wasn't for the purpose of the film, but still, I was getting paid for visiting the place, like everything else during this trip. From the start, this visit intrigued me. I couldn't understand why they wanted to take me to some strange nightclub. I asked many times for more details, but Momo would not answer me.

All I knew was that every expense was paid for and I had an open bar. Fantastic, right? In different circumstances, it would be very appealing, but somehow it made me feel even more skeptical. Momo and the whole crew came along, with the exception of Yuka, for the first time.

The club was a high end, classy place. Going by appearance, it looked more like a fancy bar with a small dance floor. The lighting was low and the atmosphere was intimate. Everyone was well dressed and the place was full of very elegant Japanese women.

As I walked in, I watched, from the corner of my eyes, a businessman choosing two women at the bar. This is it! I knew it!! This just confirmed what I was afraid of. I concluded they wanted to offer me sexual intercourse with a Japanese girl, as a gift. Perhaps it is a cultural thing too?

I wasn't too surprised when they asked me to "choose" 3 to 4 girls at the bar. Wait. Why "four?" The girls took a good long look at me and started giggling. We bowed like crazy and we all sat around a large round table, where a bartender brought us four bottles of champagne.

Two of the dolls sat on my right and the other two on my left. They surrounded me. None of the girls spoke English but they were still talking to me like it didn't matter.

MOMO TRANSLATED as much as he could. Apparently, the subject of their conversation was my nose. How rare and beautiful it was. That was a first! I assure you, it is quite ordinary!

Everyone was drinking like a fish and the "chosen ones" seemed to have a great time. As I was the center of attention, I was honestly feeling a little lost. I kept expecting something odd to happen, but nothing ever did.

By the end of the night, all my questions were answered. As I guessed, that evening at the club was offered to me as a gift, only nothing sexual was involved. The concept of that kind of club is highly unusual for occidental people. Japanese men go there for company. They pay the girls to talk to them!

Intelligent and very beautiful, the girls are highly trained to adapt themselves very quickly to the people they have to deal with, and their job is to make the clients feel good about themselves, for up to one hour, or even all night long. Depending on what they need, they make them laugh, compliment them, and listen to them.

It makes them feel important, sometimes even attractive. Sort of like how I felt when they kept talking about my nose! The goal of every girl is to push their customers to ordering drinks, to keep the club happy, but also because they're on commission.

A French magazine made the decision to send one of their photographers, to do a report on my trip to Japan. That's when the Japanese crew and their producer got completely lost. French??? But isn't Rebecca LOAD American?? Unaware about my great disability, they were shocked, as much as I was, about the misunderstanding.

Eric, the photographer, spent a week with us and was having such a hard time adapting to the food and other things that I knew he was secretly glad not to have to stay any longer. The poor thing was begging for some pizza all day long, which was very insulting to the people I was with.

As I mentioned before, I was spoiled during my entire time in Tokyo. Aside from the numerous amounts of gifts, they took me to the best restaurants the city offered, almost every night.

The fanciest one had wonderful dishes pictured on their menu. Every course was served on its own specific homebuilt wooden boat, with decorations and ornaments. Of course, I picked the prettiest one for everyone to share.

Imagine my surprise when the waiter brought us a five-foot boat, with an enormous fish inside, still alive! The fanciest dish in Japan is a live raw fish, because it's the freshest way possible they can serve it. Which makes total sense, except I would rather see it on TV than to have to face the agonized animal moving in front of me.

The fish has already been pre-cut, for me to dish out! Its body was covered with ice, the head was right in front of me.

I told the story many times to my friends and they always thought I was exaggerating, but I am telling you: the fish was looking straight at me. His protruding eyes were staring at mine! It even occurred to me that the fish was trying to communicate, but let's not go there, you will think I'm crazy. It's not like I could have stormed the door with him under my arm, like a football running back, and run all the way to the ocean, to put him back where he belonged anyway.

As I was paralyzed by it, I was hearing the others, cheering me to have the first bite. No way was I going to eat the poor fish, even knowing it would offend them. And I just didn't. I lied with the most common excuse, saying I felt sick, which actually ended up being true, a few minutes after. I wonder why.

My sex scene in the movie was with the most popular Japanese performer at the time. I always wonder why they even bother doing sex scenes in Japan, since you can barely see the penetration as they cover pubic hair with a scrambled mosaic.

We were supposed to shoot two scenes, but I declined one of them. That particular one included mainly Japanese bondage. As custom dictates, the submissive person has to be the female and it requires her to be tied up with a large rope, in a very hard and painful way, all over her body. The chest been included, and the person is also suffocating. There were no comprises to be made for me, everyone has a limit and pain is mine.

As for the "regular" sex scene, we didn't have any directive. It felt so strange! You could compare it to two persons in a boxing ring, dropped there to do the best they could.

As an occidental, I think about sex being about the connection between one another, in a playful manner. But something was wrong and nothing I was doing worked. I tried the best I could, but not only wasn't I helping my partner, I had the feeling I was making it worse.

People around us were whispering to each other but no one was talking to us directly. They finally announced they were going to have a meeting next door for a few minutes! Nice! Not awkward at all. Unable to communicate to each other because of the language barrier, we both lit up a cigarette and admired the plain white ceiling.

Momo came back with a serious look on his face and asked to talk to me in private. What did I do?? From what he told me, apparently everything. I was moving around and constantly touching the guy!

Apparently, I wasn't supposed to. Of course, I might have thought of that, but since nobody said anything, how could I have? Momo explained how I must act, in order for the scene to happen, meaning I was to lie down passively on my back, in a completely submissive way and let him be in control of everything. Not to worry, I was able to make a little bit of noise here and there. At that instant, I felt so glad to be French and not Japanese! I complied and things went fine.

I honestly didn't mind, I was there to do a job, not to judge. What irritated me were the wasted hours I spent trying to make it work, while the director could have explained the misunderstanding right away, in five seconds. Well, maybe a little more, considering his English was as good as my Japanese.

The only thing that kept him from doing that was their concept of respect. Telling me I was doing it wrong would have been humiliating me. Then what about degrading women with bondage and submission? Evidently, this was a very different story. Welcome to Japan!

Sometimes things can't be understood if it isn't from our culture. At the end of the sex scene, when the guy is about to come, they filmed my toes! I guess it shows the pleasure the same way a face does.

When the director explained his career decision to become a porn director, he told me that first he had to be a submissive, then a dominatrix, a grip, a sound guy, then a cameraman. All this so he could fully understand his crew and be a good director.

Unlike the photo shoot, which went very smoothly and without any surprises, the dancing tour, once again, was quite the adventure! Nothing like what happened in Philadelphia. This time, it was actually more like the opposite.

Three clubs per night were scheduled. They weren't nude clubs, so I needed to keep my underwear on. My job was to tease and dance with my theme costumes. I thought teasing was about interaction, to get people's attention, combined with lots of eye contact, but guess what? Exactly, wrong again!

Customers felt assaulted! Me being too close, right in front of them, was perceived as aggression. The thing is, they weren't rude about it. They were very nice and polite, but most of all, they were tipping very generously. So, because it wasn't obvious to me at first, I thought everyone was happy! In the US, the more people tip you, the longer you stay and play with them—they enjoy what you do.

In Japan, customers were paying me to go away! They were giving me money so I would be done and leave. It took me a while to figure it out! I must confess that it's a strange feeling once you understand they want you to go away. I didn't know what to do anymore on stage. Anything I was doing seemed to scared them or piss them off. I guess it wasn't that bad after all, since the people I worked for were happy enough to organize two other venues, with almost the same schedule, the following year. The night before my departure, they threw a really nice and emotional goodbye party. More gifts, more alcohol and most of all, Yuka gave me a beautiful dress that she made herself especially for me.

When could she have found the time to do it? She was with me 18 hours a day, every day. It seemed impossible! She smiled and answered that she did it during her sleeping time.

ANYBODY THAT THINKS they work too much needs to go to Japan. They would surely feel different about it. I honestly don't know how anybody can survive such a heavy rhythm of work. I don't envy them, but I have to admit that I admire them for it.

I really enjoyed my trip in Japan. It was a unique opportunity and I was glad to have done it. But my weeks there were so intense, I was just glad to go home. I was beat! I flew back with Japanese bills hidden all over me, mostly under my clothes. I had Japanese yen in my blouse, bra and my shoes. That same year, I won the Japanese Award for Best "American" Actress.

I love those guys!

Chapter 14

NOT TOO LONG AFTER I came back from Japan, I had the opportunity to meet, and work, for a very well-known company: Adam & Eve. I've rarely seen so many wonderful, smiling, discreet and well-educated persons in one place! I wondered if it was a requirement to be hired in the company, or if they all were part of the same family!

I got to know Bob Christian a little better, who is one of the big kahunas there. During stressful times, like conventions for example, Bob and I were often seeking each other for some hugs. It quickly became a game. Some people take coffee breaks, I was taking hug breaks!

The way their team presented themselves reflected their products, as their reputation was based on good judgment and class. Their concept was unique, and they had no competition. They are very respected by everyone, even by the civilian's mainstream newspapers and magazines, Adam & Eve is one of the rare adult companies able to advertise in regular magazines and newspapers.

They are the symbol of respected porn fights for freedom of speech and the right to contraceptives. Even the ACLU speaks out for them.

Nadine Strossen, then-president of the American Civil Liberties Union, wrote, "Phil Harvey not only survived the government's relentless efforts to bully him out of business, as it had done to other businesspeople who also sold constitutionally protected materials to adults who sought those materials. Even more inspiringly, Phil Harvey and his impressive legal team secured new legal precedents and prosecutorial policies that will protect other individuals and businesses from similar government harassment and oppression."

What this means is that without him, none of "us" would be here. Based in North Carolina, far away from the rest of the Adult World, they are the largest mail-order company in the US.

I was once invited by my Hug-buddy to visit their office and warehouse in North Carolina. The whole thing was mind-blowing. Their mailing network was gigantic. They even had their own railroad track going into the warehouse. A regular post office couldn't even dream of it! Everything was thought of, even their own envelopes, which were thick and discreet.

As I was given the big tour, I was all ears, just like I was inside a museum. I learned a lot about the US that day.

Like how you can't ship adult products to every state because some prohibit it, or even worst, you can ship to some states but not some counties, and I learned simply what some people went through in the US to allow the adult industry to exist.

So many fights over the years and there still are today, so much Puritanism and restrictions related to sex or nudity. How contradictory in a country that produces more adult films than anywhere else in the world!

Why is the US adult world the largest by far? You would think it would be Europe, for example, where there is much more acceptance towards nudity and sex.

Of course, there is always the business part of it to be considered. When there is a substantial profit to be made (it is a 3 billion dollar industry), Americans are better than anyone else at it. Is that really it?

In my experience, I truly doubt it. It isn't only about porn. Think of strip clubs for example. Why aren't they successful in Europe, unlike over here, where there are so many of them?

I believe that has to do with us, as human beings. Any restriction or prohibition creates more need compared to places where there isn't any. Putting something within everyone's reach makes it ordinary, with less value.

Did you know that the biggest number of adult film consumers are in Utah? A state where you could be arrested for carrying a porn magazine in the trunk of your car!

The same people who officially preach against nudity sometimes are the same ones that watch porn at night, behind closed doors. Some call it "hypocrisy," but I think it's more complicated than it seems. Guilt over behavior that is against your education or religious belief might be one of the reasons.

As I travelled all over the US for promotional purposes, I went many times to Texas. One of the video stores I was assigned to had burned down four times in 2 years. Each time, mysteriously, in the middle of the night. I was so impressed by its owner, a tiny old man with puppy eyes, who wouldn't let those events intimidate him. He'd re-built each time, and probably many times after!

Store signings were so unpredictable to me. It was impossible to know how it would turn out in advance.

It is very different from conventions. There, individuals could disappear into the crowd and lose their identity. The intimacy of a store makes the approach more personal. Over a full day of signing, you can't expect to have the store crowded the entire time, as the fans often arrived in waves.

It was during down times that I could witness the most interesting attitudes. More than once, I thought the store was almost empty, and then realized that some people were hiding in the store's aisles, behind videos and DVDs. The more I encouraged them to come closer, the more they seemed to disappear. I wondered what they actually looked like and what position they took to be invisible that fast!

One in particular distinguished himself from the others. He was very well hidden behind a shelf, looking at me through two videotapes. All I could see was one eye staring. Try and picture it. Stalker alert!

As for the most reckless ones that weren't hiding, some were dragging their feet looking down at the floor. Others were staring at magazine covers for a whole 10 minutes.

At this point, you only need one to dare to make the first step. Once it's done, the others generally follow. I never got over that kind of behavior. I see myself as someone friendly, at least most of the time.

"Nine and a Half Weeks" was a video store chain, and they signed me up a couple of times in different locations. The last time I worked for them was with J.R Carrington. The owner tricked us into a dinner with four of his clients. Since he left us with no alternative, I decided to ruin the dinner by being in a terrible mood and "give the look" at anyone who tried to talk to me. The benefit of that was, in case any other person thought to surprise us without our consent, like having a "lucky night," they'd probably think twice about it!

This experience aside, store signings were mainly fun. The most interesting thing was getting to meet different kinds of people.

I don't necessarily mean the fans, but store owners as well. Their positions are unique, since they know so much about the adult industry, without really being in it. They are professionally involved in the porn world, but indirectly. Basically, they are half civilians!

Like those two owners/associates in Boston who had a sex shop and a very successful car wash business. They were well organized and managed to do both at the same time, rotating between the two of them. I can't remember why Rick (my roadie and friend) was with me during that trip, but he was. Their welcoming was wonderful and they treated us like kings. Our time there was so special, like two friends who invited us to stay a few extra days, at their expense, for a vacation! You rarely get that kind of proposal! Sadly, California was calling my name back home.

Another store experience that can't be forgotten was in New Orleans. The owner was a man named Dudley; his nickname was "Big Daddy." He was tall and imposing, fun to be around, and extroverted by nature. He had only one goal (or should I say "obsession") while I was there—making me fall in love with his city.

I was in town for two and a half days, with only four hours of store signings. Big Daddy's mission was fully scheduled. In less than 24 hours, I knew his entire family and friends, which seemed to be ¾ of the town's population! I visited New Orleans from A to Z at the speed of light.

Something caught my attention almost right away. Everywhere we went, my precious guide wasn't paying for anything. Restaurant owners always personally welcomed him, in bars or nightclubs, food and drinks were free! Since Big Daddy wanted me to see the maximum amount possible of the city, we weren't staying in one spot more than 15 or 20 minutes each time. Just enough to consume something and be on our way.

The whole thing was very nice and I felt privileged, but being under the impression that the entire city knew him, it was a bit strange. It isn't like New Orleans is a small town! I ended up wondering with whom I was really hanging out. Needless to say, I kept my wondering to myself! Bottom line, mission accomplished: how could I not love New Orleans after such a treat? The place itself is already magic.

I went back twice to New Orleans. Once with Philippe, during one of our annual road trips, crossing the US. I insisted he meet Dudley, and as I planned, he made such an impression on my husband, it was hilarious. Big Daddy could care less that our visit wasn't for professional reasons and he proudly gave us the big tour again. We ate so much crawfish I am surprised I didn't became one myself.

We only missed one lunch with him. Unexpectedly, Big Daddy was almost an hour late. I guess his excuse was valid—you can't really blame someone being late because one of his friends got shot, cold blooded, in the street, that same morning! If you think that kind of news is scary, I assure you it wasn't the scariest. It was frightening though the way he announced it, like it was an ordinary event. Like you would mention to someone that your wife just got the flu.

As for my numerous signings in New York City, my first one was for Zakir. His nickname was Tony, even though he was from India and doesn't exactly look like an Indian. Zakir used to be a taxi driver in NYC during his early years. Apparently, being a taxi driver required multitasking while driving. Eating, being on the phone, and talking to the passenger behind you, all at the same time. If you're trying to visualize it, yes, I confirm, you can't do it with only two hands. He was using his knees to steer the bottom of the wheel. The hyper little guy, who had a great personality, was the same way in business and was running, as an associate, a very large variety of stores, including food stores and restaurants. He was everywhere at the same time, night and day. He was the kind of person who makes you feel tired just by looking at him. He introduced me to his best friend Jeff who was a vice cop in Manhattan. We all really got along very well and I came to visit them many times after, over the years, during holidays or business trips.

Of course, being there during vacation time is a major plus, since it gave me all the time I needed to enjoy it. I fell in love with New York City. I could never get enough of it. This city is incredible. It has a soul, I could feel it, I swear! I thought about moving there more than once, but never did for business reasons. The adult industry is mainly on the other coast. I hope to own a little apartment in New York one day.

Anyway, one time, Philippe was hired to do a full report on Rebecca Lord in the United States. We took the opportunity of being in New York that month, to do the pictures there as well. We did topless in front of the Manhattan Bridge and in a bikini in front of the Statue of Liberty. Our best picture was in Times Square. On a Saturday night, around 11 p.m., the place was packed, lots of police officers. I went there naked under my coat and I opened it, wide, with a large smile on my face, in front of thousands of people. Philippe wanted a powerful shot. I think he got it!

What completely blew our minds was the people's reaction. Everyone gathered, stared and applauded! Police included! You do the same in Los Angeles, you better have a good lawyer, or have special running skills.

As we were telling the story to our friends over dinner, Jeff came up with a great idea. Let's fake an arrest! How could we not have thought of it? Great pictures for the magazine! Sure enough, we organized the setup of Jeff's police car the next day, in front of the Manhattan Bridge. Jeff came with another cop and Zac's job was security, keeping the people away. As for Jeff and his friend, all dressed up in their uniforms, they posed with me, while I was handcuffed half naked, half crying. They even pushed the scenario a little further, by having me face down on the car's hood. The pictures had fantastic realism! And we had so much fun doing it.

Chapter 15

AS TIME PASSED, I gradually started to direct and produce more. Of course I was still doing movies as a performer, but less frequently. I didn't really plan it that way. Things came naturally as opportunities came to me.

I decided to co-produce movies with my friend Ron (AKA Jon Yuma), by the end of the '90s. Ron and I ran across each other many times over the years, on sets, without really connecting. Until one day, I saw him depressed because he had broken up with his long-term girlfriend who was an adult performer named Christy Lake. His love for his ex-girlfriend touched me.

The irony was that Nic was in the same condition, at the exact same period of time, also with an adult actress. I decided to introduce the two of them, so they could hang out together and share whatever needed to be shared in that kind of situation. Touching the bottom of the ocean with someone makes you feel understood and less lonely.

Earlier in life, Ron was based in Minnesota, where he was a successful consultant. He dropped his career to be in L.A. with his girlfriend. That said, he started to produce adult films and made a name for himself.

Our friendship built up over the years, even though Ron was traumatized for life during one Thanksgiving we invited him over. We had some "technical problems" with our dinner and we finally all ended up at a sushi restaurant. Far from realizing I had committed a crime that day ("No turkey? Who eats sushi on Thanksgiving?!"), he still reminds me about it, even today, every year on the occasion!

The more I was producing movies, the more my house looked like a porn cave. Between the fan club products and movie props, hiding everything became a real challenge.

The grand finale was when I received boxes of dildos from Doc Johnson, a sex toys manufacturer. I contacted them for the first movie I produced, *Pure Sex*, so they could provide me with a few of their latest toys in exchange for publicity.

I was astonished by their generosity—they sent boxes filled with every kind of sex toy. Everything you could have thought of was there; things you never thought of were there as well. Anything for singles, couples, homosexuals, SM, and things I still can't figure out what they were for, even years after. Some of them should really come with a manual.

As for the power of choice, Doc Johnson thought about it for you. Depending on your mood or dress code that day, you could even choose between a large variety of colors! Pink is too girly, especially when you wish to use it on your boyfriend? Take the dark gray one. Unless the brown one will match better with his skin tone, of course.

Being a producer made me discover things about my personality I wasn't aware of. I have a hard time letting other people have responsibilities. I desperately need to control things all the time, which makes things difficult since I can't do everything myself.

Evidently, when there was a job that required a qualification or special skill I didn't have, it made things easier since I didn't have any choice but to trust someone else. As a result of my behavior, I was a production manager, producer, director and a make-up artist. I was also often talent, as I often performed in my movies, all at the same time.

Philippe was my stills photographer and he instinctively helped more and more when I was overworked. As we got more experienced, we found out that we complemented one another on a set. He was more technical and I was more into the artwork and organization. So we naturally ended up making the movies together after a while.

We even tried to distribute a movie ourselves instead of handing it out to a distributor. That didn't go very well! I went door to door presenting my movie and even though company owners welcomed me warmly, I could sense my approach caused much surprise. Most of them bought between 2 and 15 movies, which literally meant they made a noble gesture, to be on friendly terms with me. They thought that was cute!! "Cute" wasn't exactly what I was looking for! "Cute" doesn't qualify as being taken seriously.

It wasn't the proper way to do business. Movies had to go through distributors, as they have special deals with adult companies. It was policy. There were people on payroll called "buyers" for a reason.

In fact, distributors have a list with very specific client names on it. I call it the "secret list," since it remains kind of secret and has a very high value. How naïve of me to have thought for a second it could be done differently!

Some say there isn't number two without number 3. This is exactly what happened with my dancing career. Friends and colleagues kept telling me how unlucky I was to have started at that club in Philly. That I basically started at the worst one, that it didn't represent the dancing experience at all. Others even insisted that feature dance was an amazing experience that truly completed an adult porn star's career. It was hard for me to imagine, but the fact that everyone around me was saying the exact same thing bothered me.

Fine then. I agreed to give it another chance, but this time, I was going to choose carefully, with recommendations, which club I was going to be at. First, I wanted it to be in the L.A. area, where I lived, and it had to be for a very short period of time, like a weekend thing.

So I decided to do it for a couple of nights. An unexpected and amazing thing happened during those two nights… everything went well! The club was happy, customers were happy, I was happy! Happy ending. Everyone lived happy ever after!

It was an experience that suddenly changed my career and my life, since I found myself going on the road for the next six years, off and on. "Going on the road" for a porn star means extending her film career. Like I explained before, the more exposed or famous a talent becomes, the longer she lasts, but it also means facing the real world.

She can't hide behind a camera anymore. A bubble, created by the adult world, doesn't protect her. And most of all, she can't come home after work like nothing happened, leading a double life.

Feature dancing is a way to take full responsibility for being an adult actress. You meet people and fans to talk about your job, to show them the living fantasy. That's what you are there for and that's all they want to hear about.

By doing that, you realize through them what you do for a living. This is not to be confused with realizing who you are, which has nothing to do with the job you do.

We are a marketing product. If a few adult film stars don't quite realize that, it is also true that some fans think we *are* "it." Not only we are a product, but also we are a fantasy. Basically, we are what people want us to be.

Who we are, is meaningless, we aren't real. It takes character and a meaningful private life on the side to help know who we are and restore the balance. To be the ones that don't get lost easily and never fall into the darkness.

Fame can get to your head and make you do stupid things. Hence the importance of having a REAL private life that has nothing to do with your job; this is ideal for anyone, for that matter. If you're a cowboy, you don't bring your horse into your home.

Those six years (and more) of dancing tours in the US were very enlightening. From my perspective, a strip club looks awfully like a subway. Depending on the tram and the hours, it's more crowded than others. You can see, and meet, any kind of people, all generations, all nationalities and social classes. Naïve are the people who believe, like I did, a long, long time ago, that there is only one kind of customer that goes to strip clubs!

A person who works in a strip joint learns very quickly how to distinguish one type of customer from another. It doesn't take long to recognize the real spenders as opposed to the ones who fake it to attract the girls, for example. On the other hand, it's also easy to recognize a new stripper from the others. She would be the one that goes straight away to the customer wearing a suit, thinking he has more money. This is the classic trap that one falls into after one week in a strip club!

Dark as it might be, the club has eyes. Everything is organized and watched. They make you feel like you're alone with a girl but in fact, it's teamwork. Drinks are shared between the club and the strippers, lap dances too, stage dances with the D.J., and so on. Some girls even work as a team without anyone noticing. It's a way to have extra protection, or to exchange customers when one is too busy. It is impressive.

These are the typical types of customers:

The regulars. They love being known by every girl in the club, being called by their first name and being hugged by the girls as they walk in. They usually have their "favorite" stripper and they are very faithful.

The occasional. You can tell them by the way they look at the girls as they arrive. They look right away for the one who might make their night worth coming.

The first timer. Like a 5 year old at Disneyland! He might also just look like a cartoon character, with hearts replacing his eyes and a flow of little stars coming out of his mouth.

There is also the type that actually thinks the strippers like him, and that he might go home with one of us. Believe me, this basically never happens.

As I met my fans during signings, after each show performance, I was so relieved to have been the one that personally took care of my fan club. It allowed me to remember some of my fans, which made a tremendous difference in my line of work. That is, when they took the time to introduce themselves, instead of just coming up to me, saying, "Hi Rebecca, it's ME, Steve!" expecting a hug like we were best friends.

It's a fact—Steve is a very rare first name in the US, like Michael or John! Reflexes aren't always controlled by your brain, and in this case, for example, my education was that instead of just saying things that could hurt their feelings, I found myself responding instantly, "Oh hiiiiiiiii! How are youuu!" Which put me in an awkward position for the following half hour while I hoped they would talk long enough for me to realize who they were.

I learned to actually enjoy stripping on stage, whether the crowd was supportive or not. When people from the club work with you as a team, they create lighting effects adapted to the type of music you hand them, and even manage to have shadows to hide your imperfections, if requested. DJs always say the greatest things about you on the microphone, while you're on stage and some customers are cheering you. It makes you feel sexy. Yes, let's call a cat a cat—it is totally narcissistic!

I have to admit to not being the easiest feature dancer clubs ever worked with. I was messy. My shows always ended up having something special as the last song, which required a lot of cleaning before house girls could put a foot on stage. Whipped cream rubbed against my body would not have been such a mess if I didn't have the idea to roll over on the floor everywhere right after. As for the cute bubble machine that I enjoyed putting behind me, which gave a nicer mood to the show, I had to get rid of it. I can't believe that stuff contained soap. They should write that stuff on the bottle in big letters. Who knew? And then of course there were the bad jokes like "slippery when wet!"

But still, I heard the worst from them in my most creative show: The "Milk Bath." At the end of the 3rd song, Rick would bring a plastic pool on stage for me to use, along with 2 gallons of milk and one of those big outdoor water guns filled up with milk as well. After a few sexy poses in my pool, pouring milk all over me, I would hand the gun to whoever was motivated to shoot me with it.

Of course, the fun part was to have him miss, which involved shooting anywhere in the room, or even better, at the person across the stage, by mistake. Some of the victims had their revenge, as the gun passed from hand to hand and I vividly remember a few that were shooting right at each other, shamelessly, while I patiently waited—naked—on stage.

Even if Rick did the best he could to clean up as much as possible after me, he was limited to the stage area and by time as well, since other girls were waiting to take the stage.

My mess could have spoiled my relationship with the house girls, but it didn't, for some reason. Most of the time, I was warmly welcomed and they were nice to us all along. I am aware that feature dancers are usually welcomed, since they are supposed to bring more customers to the club, meaning more money for the strippers. But still, adult film stars have different experiences.

Knowing that some jealous girls would criticize, no matter what, I just nicely kept a minimum distance from all of them, just in case. After all, we were only passing through and they were in their work element.

It is a strange thing, but a fact that I was booked way more often on the East Coast than any other part of the country. I really can't be sure why, but my guess is that it had something to do with my look. I don't quite have the California girl's figure. I am not a blonde with big boobs.

It was always really exciting to come to New York City. Most of the strip clubs there were handled by Italians, which I especially get along with pretty well. I liked the way things, like club rules, were straightforward from the beginning, which helped avoid any misunderstandings. Clearly, respecting their rules was all they asked for, which made for a friendly relationship anywhere I went.

Rick certainly helped socially during my dancing trips. He is the easiest person to talk to and get along with. Officially, his job was bodyguard, which always makes me laugh since he couldn't hurt a fly. It wasn't obvious at first sight, since he physically looked more like a line backer than Woody Allen. I was just hoping that was enough to keep ill-intentioned people away, or that they would avoid talking to him long enough to figure it out. Overall, it worked pretty well!

I only walked away from a club twice. Doing something like that, before my contract ended, meant it really had to be a very bad experience.

One was in Manhattan, at a very "high end," luxurious gentleman's club, with a great reputation, handled by Russian people. I had a bad feeling from the start. I kept asking to meet the manager or the owner, but in vain. Their assistants handled every exchange we had. The manager's office was always locked, with two cameras pointing at me when I knocked, but no one ever opened the door. That's cold. Cold and weird.

Everyone from the club was ignoring us, even the house girls. It felt like we weren't welcome at all, but we couldn't understand why. Until one night, as I walked past the manager's office, the door wasn't shut correctly and left enough space for me to witness a situation.

A stripper was crying loudly, begging a man to spare her from having sex with a specific client. There is no need to go into details, but the person being spoken to didn't exactly care about how she felt and wasn't giving her any choice. I was horrified. No one saw me and I quietly went back to my dressing room.

As I explained the event to Rick we realized that the apartment building adjoining the Club belonged to them as well. Most of the strippers were Russians that didn't speak any English. Everything suddenly became crystal clear. The strip club was mainly a front! Such a place made it impossible for me to stay any longer.

But things were complicated. I couldn't exactly just sneak out without being seen. I had to cross the entire club and pass a dozen club assistants to get to the front door, and that was if I decided to leave all my stuff behind AND run away without civilian's clothes on. I was stuck. Of course, I could have waited until the next day and just never showed up again, but leaving everything behind bothered me. Plus, getting paid for the work I did gave me extra motivation.

Which left Rick in utter dismay. There was no other option but to confront them face-to-face. I wasn't too comfortable about the idea of pissing them off, which meant I had to find a reason, other than revealing the truth I knew about them.

I certainly didn't want to create a paranoid reaction or make them believe I was going to the police. We decided quickly—the plan was for Rick to wait outside, in case something bad happened, then he would be able to call for help. I had half an hour before he would.

When I announced to one of the assistants I wanted to leave, two others joined him in a heartbeat. The leader made me repeat it. He was looking straight at me, fixing my eyes without blinking. If I had had an ounce of humor left in me that day, I would have asked if he was playing that silly game where the first one who blinks loses the game.

But instead I said, "I don't like your club, that's why, please pay what you owe me." No answer. No one moved or reacted. We stayed silent for several seconds. It seemed like an eternity. Then I added, "Friends are already waiting for me outside." Far from been impressed by it, he smiled and left the room. The two body builders with identical black leather jackets stayed with me until Mr. Never-Blink came back with my money. He looked at me again, like he was searching for my soul, and never exchanged one word with me. There is absolutely no doubt that he knew the real reason for my departure. We both knew it.

The next day I called my NYPD friend, Jeff. I never found out what happened afterwards.

The second club where I refused to honor my contract with was in El Paso, Texas. It was owned by two old ladies that I believe were sisters. It was really impossible to tell how old they were, since they had done so much plastic surgery. One of them in particular reminded me of that woman from the movie *Brazil* by Terry Gilliam. Those two made quite a team. You could tell, by their team's behavior, that they were bullies.

The club was unusually dark and I could barely make it to my dressing room without banging into tables or chairs. The funny thing was, you couldn't really see the strippers unless they were two feet in front of you. Someone please explain to me what's the point of that in a strip club?

The sisters quickly became a problem. They never took the time to sign my contract. They were always postponing it for later, which isn't the way things are done. Contracts are to be signed before the job starts. I did my first show without it, then my second, and then I stopped. We got into a fight as they were still feeding me pretexts to avoid signing any agreement. I understood they were hoping to rip me off. I slammed the door and never looked back.

Six months later, the sisters were all over Texas newspapers. They got arrested for employing underage girls, mainly Mexican immigrants. No wonder the club was so dark! No one could tell how old the girls were. A couple of months after, the club was found burnt down to the ground. How strange!

It was such a major contrast with strip clubs where everything goes smoothly. Especially with the ones that really come close to perfection, at any level. A few clubs come to my mind, but one was above all of them was near Lincoln, Nebraska. It's very simple—it had been my most enjoyable AND lucrative Club experience ever, managed by fantastic people. Nebraska, how unexpected!

The owner came to pick us up at the airport himself, with an old pickup truck. Their welcome was warm and sincere. They seemed really thrilled to have us there, all week long. I got a little confused at first, when we parked in front of a field full of cows though.

Even more when I understood that the huge shed on the other side of it was the strip club! This club was family owned with a friendly atmosphere. Everyone got along with each other and they seemed happy to work there, strippers included.

It was so refreshing. As for the club itself, it was packed all week long. There was not enough space for people to sit down, but that didn't affect their enthusiasm. Some of them showed up with huge banners written: "Welcome Rebecca Lord," cheering me until they had no voices anymore.

When I think of it, I guess I might have been the only event in the region for quite a while! That's the thing, in a small town, any tiny event could bring an excess of joy, in contrast to a big city where anything goes on and where people aren't impressed that easily. That place, right there, in the middle of nowhere, is the perfect example.

Bottom line: I was "it." The owner also explained that the club was one of a kind for this location at the crossroads of Nebraska, Iowa and Kansas. There was no other strip joint for miles around, so customers would then drive from all over this big area to get to his place, and then, stay overnight.

I sold out every single thing I had to sell in the first three days. I ended up selling parts of my dancing costumes for customers that begged for it.

I chose my dancing tours to be only once every four to six weeks. Going out for several weeks in a row, or a few months like some performers do, wasn't the kind of life I was looking for.

I did try it once, and that experience really proved I wasn't fit for it. I went on a four-week tour of eight clubs for a strip club chain on the East Coast called. "Déjà vu."

Technically, everything went fine, but the whole thing was just too much for me, physically and mentally. After a while, I could only see people's loneliness and nothing else. Even if all kinds of people were visiting strip clubs, I would say that 70% of them (if I had to put a number on it) had one thing in common. They were coming to the clubs to forget about whatever is wrong in their lives. It could be loneliness or just the special need of a getaway. Some of them like to talk about it, and some others demonstrate it to you by their attitudes. Our job is to make them forget or listen to them, when needed. I say "our," because strippers and features are in the same boat on this one. The status is meaningless. It is easy to take a few steps back when it's for a short time, but too much of it, for a long period of time, affected me.

I am not ashamed to admit I wasn't built for it and that was my weak point. Everyone has a weak point. Do not be mistaken. I had nothing against hearing some "confessions" about their lives or problems, quite the contrary. I am actually happy and proud to have contributed, somehow, in a very small way, to helping people to feel better, even for a few minutes or a few hours. I care too much and my shoulders aren't big enough, that's all.

The "magic time" for conversation happens during the lap dances, because of its privacy. People were paying for several dances in a row just so they could talk to me in private. Of course it wasn't always the case and many customers asked for real lap dances!

Doing lap dances for a feature entertainer wasn't mandatory. It was up to me to accept or not. I enjoyed it and only rarely refused it. I never had a bad experience or at least bad enough for me to remember it. I simply avoided customers under the influence of alcohol or who were just too wired. Being an adult film star doesn't help people to behave. Because of our status and because they pay a higher price for the dance, some of them hope to get more than just a tease. The balance between being sensual and in control of the situation at the same time wasn't always easy to do.

Doing a lap dance is quite unique. It's a strange feeling that could sometimes even be exciting for both parties. In less than two seconds, both people are thrown to an intimate universe that ends in three minutes. It's a brief exchange. Very powerful. If I am the only one that loses my clothes, the customer, on the other hand, is the one that loses his mask. It falls off. His eyes betray him. Sometimes their entire facial expression changes, or even a sudden bump appears between their legs.

Some feminists don't get it. Strippers aren't the victims—they are the ones with the power!

Being far away from home, Rick and I tried to fill in our afternoons the best we could. We visited a lot of places, when possible, which wasn't always the case, depending on how far away our hotel was from the city. We usually had to be back at the club by 6 p.m., which only left us a few hours to spare. Since our bedtime was around 7 a.m., we used the "Do Not Disturb" sign all mornings. I love hotel staff when they conscientiously call you at 10 a.m., wondering if you need anything. "Are you sure?"

To give you an idea of how boring life was, outside the club, when we were in the middle of nowhere, our favorite activity was to watch the worst TV possible. We used to call them the "Z" movies. The typical low budget action movie, where the good guys always win, the bad ones always die, and in between, a "babe" with big boobs runs everywhere. The worse the movie was, the funnier for us. The more dialogue that was meant to be serious, the more it was hilarious to watch. Porn actors couldn't do a worse acting job. It's impressive how silly two 25 to 30-year-old kids can become when they are bored. I still can't believe we did the most immature things ever.

It was hard to keep occupied. We sent anonymous letters to David (the photographer/paparazzi) with cut out words from newspapers, knowing he gets easily paranoid, just for the fun of it. We would decorate a friend's car with shaving cream and then wait for hours in the bushes to see a reaction.

Extreme fatigue? Stress relief? I like to blame it on not enough cable TV. I apologize to people who read this and believe a porn star is always having orgies or such in her spare time. Nothing that fancy here!

Philippe and I bought a book directory for strip clubs in the US. We wanted to travel across the country, once a year, to visit some clubs, as we'd be in the area. The purpose was to leave pictures and résumés when I visited a club I liked, which was a great way to control where to perform.

This was the best idea we ever had. We saw things I would never have thought existed. We wound up in farms laid out as a clubs, large dining halls where girls danced on tables between plates (I recommend their chicken breast, by the way) or, yes, believe it or not, a club in a gas station!

Too bad we didn't have Smartphone's at that time. I would have discreetly taken pictures as proof. The tiny gas station had a larger than usual cashier counter, and that was the stage. There was blue lighting on the ceiling. There was a 50-year-old dancer on the stage that wasn't too motivated. She broke my heart, so I gave her a tip. That's when she smiled in return and I wish she didn't. Her front teeth missing still haunt me at night.

I know that I said it before but this country just blows my mind. So much diversity, so much contradiction. I think that is what makes it so interesting and so lovable.

Before most performances, it was customary to be invited to be on a local radio station, to drag more people to the club. I was aware that it was beneficial for business and I made the effort to appear when requested, even if I was reluctant to do it in some cases.

I was glad to have had several experiences beforehand with TV networks and radio stations with my friend April from Spice. I was so hung up about my English, which was weak at the beginning, so she always found a way for me to go live with a co-worker. My first radio interview, for example, was in Tucson, Arizona.

I was petrified when the crew told me the entire show was based on live calls from fans! Marc Davis, one of my favorite actors, was with me that day, and helped me get through it in a very clever way. He purposely was answering first, even if they were questions that were meant to be for me, in a humorous tone.

And then, it's like almost anything in life: you get used to it. You just have to adapt your attitude according to the type of radio show you are on, which also depends on which state and city you are in.

I went to a Catholic radio show in Dallas, Texas once. I went on right after the Mayor's live interview. Questions were soft and casual, asked in between religious songs!

However, the following month, I did the entire weather forecast, topless. Listeners certainly couldn't see me, but the team from the show made so many comments, that it was almost like everyone was there.

In Buffalo, Niagara Falls the challenge was to simulate an orgasm. The team was so disgusted by its authenticity, they all swore during the show never to buy a porn movie ever in their life. Their fantasies went to trash.

Most of the time, I always heard the same comment, over and over. People from the show didn't expect to see me as I was. That I didn't physically reflect the cliché of a porn star. If that remark is true and could be to my advantage in my private life, it wasn't on a radio show. Those guys provoked me more than other performers, on purpose, to see if I was the "real deal."

In New York City, the *Howard Stern Show* was and still is a very notorious and successful show that aimed to provoke. Broadcast on radio and TV, any kind of subject was game: politics, religion, music, porn, health, etc. Howard was arrogant and a provocateur like no one else. People loved the "king of media" for those 2 characteristics.

I wanted to be on the show so badly to advertise my website! Unfortunately, the more popular a show is, the more difficult it is to be on the list of future guests, especially when I had no one behind me, like a famous production company or an agent, to give me a push.

I wasn't going to wait for miracles, so I decided to show up unexpectedly one morning. The worst that could happen was being kicked out, which honestly was the most likely outcome.

But no! It was apparently a slow morning to them and they could easily make some extra time for me to be on the show. I was prepared to be eaten alive by Mr. Stern, which was a common practice with his porn star guests, that aren't even French! It was the opposite! I was astonished by his respectful attitude towards me. I was even offered to stay longer and went on his next show, a TV show that followed called The Gay Family Feud. My part wasn't too exiting and didn't quite make me look very smart, but I gladly accepted.

For the entire show, I wore a bathing suit while everyone else was dressed like a New Yorker in winter. My job was to follow Mr. Stern, as if I was glued to him. I laughed when required, and said a long difficult phrase, once: "Yes!"

In exchange for playing the bimbo, Howard mentioned my website address, twice, during his show. I would do it again in a heartbeat, every day of the year. I got 3 million hits on my website that day! Rick called me from home later on to congratulate me and also to announce my server burnt down. What a disaster. We weren't prepared for so many hits. Which wasn't the case when I decided to go back a year later!

Shameless, I showed up the same way, and even though they had politely asked me to stop coming uninvited, they let me go back on again. My server held this time. 8 million hits came through with success. I stopped bothering Howard Stern after that! Although I believe it might have been a perfect timing for not coming back anytime soon. That last appearance was particularly notable for comments I and Howard made about the Catholic Church which led the Catholic League for Religious and Civil Rights to call for Miller Brewing to drop its sponsorship of the show. Oooops!

My fan club took another turn, and I found myself quite busy looking after it. The postman behind the counter got used to seeing me every day holding packages. After a while we were even sharing music suggestions. When the line was too long, he would come to me and put his headphones on my ears. Funny guy.

Chapter 16

AS TIME PASSED, I was looking for a way to bring something a little more exciting than just goodies to purchase on my website.

What motivated me was when I realized how crazy people went after little things that were more original than others. I had comic books made by two cartoonists. One was based on my real life, my religious education included, and evolved quickly to provocations and sexual fantasies. On the other hand, the second one was pure fantasy; it was the adventuress Rebecca Lord, with a black suit and a motorcycle. I was half Terminator, half Catwoman. My mission was saving the world, by having lots of sex. I know, don't hold it against me, I only chose the cartoonist!

I was looking for something more personal. Live cam was in development, but it meant making appointments that I wasn't able to keep most of the time. I then had the idea of offering phone sex. People aren't stupid. They know that most of the time the girl on the other side of the phone isn't always what she pretends to be. The advantage I had was my accent. People knew they weren't being lied to.

People who ordered phone sex were fans, for the most part, but not always. It was a real blind adventure for each phone call, and not one person was identical. I cannot possibly imagine phone sex ever becoming something boring for the woman who does it professionally, even after several years. The diversity of requests is just too impressive.

It inevitably has to do with the fact that suddenly people feel free of any judgment. They feel some kind of absolute protection and anonymity, hiding behind their phones.

As far as I'm concerned, that attitude towards me was purely psychological. To place a phone sex order through my site, it required having their full name, address and credit card number. Not too anonymous, if you ask me! Which really means, not being able to see one another is enough to give that fake impression.

Bottom line: I heard everything that could possibly be heard. When a phone conversation was too insane, I would either let them talk and stopped participating or I would end the call. But at the beginning, I found myself hesitating from hanging up. That's when I heard way too much than needed. Like, for example, having someone ask me to take on the role of a child molester, raping my own kid until he actually loved it and begged for more. You should have seen my face the first time. I hung up furiously.

Wait, it gets better. There was a whole script where I am in a cemetery, digging corpses from their graves, helping out my caller to make love to them, as I practiced anal sex on the dead bodies with a heavy religious cross. The whole masquerade went on for quite a long time, while we sang out loud how much we loved Priest (whatever). For some reason, I can't remember his name at this time. This one wasn't only crazy, he was scary.

I then felt obligated to act, and I have no regrets to having called the FBI on him. I just couldn't live with myself knowing I had information on someone that disturbing, and then acting like it didn't matter. Like Rick said, "If they are someday seeking a serial killer in that particular state, at least they'll know where to look!"

Playing a "character" in a small script was quite common. I would become someone they imagined being with, like an existing person, an imaginary one or even myself in a situation they chose. Especially when that person was a regular. The script either changed with each phone call, or was the same one over and over. My part was to understand very quickly what the person was expecting from me. I found it sexy at times, depending on who I was talking to.

I had to listen carefully the first couple of minutes to figure out who I was dealing with, and then adapt the best I could, according to their needs. That is, if the person talked or we had a conversation, some of them just stayed silent. Try and find out what to say when the other person doesn't even answer your questions! Lonely times. "Are you still there? Allo? Allo?!"

Doing phone sex with regulars was a strange thing as well. After a while, I got to know some of them pretty well, without ever having met them in real life. I knew their apartments by heart from their descriptions, their colleagues' names from work, their cats' names, their favorite book or TV series, what they bought for Christmas, and so on. At the beginning, I had to write down everything! I was afraid to confuse one person with another. Imagine asking someone how was work today to someone who lost his job, or a football player how was his game last week to a handicapped person! A lot of them were ordering phone calls to talk about anything for the most part, and we'd have a brief sex conversation at the end, just to make it official.

I confess that I even started caring for a few of them, and I believe that in different circumstances, we could have become friends at some point. Phone sex is also a way, commonly used, for lonely people to connect with a human being who will not judge.

The fact that some fans were very friendly gave me the idea to create my own radio show. Entirely "homemade," through my website, it was fun, but not well organized. Once a week, at night, the concept was to take live phone calls, with music in between. With a few exceptions, the same people were there all the time, and the show became a fun meeting between everyone. Although strangers to each other at first, they ended up knowing one another and quickly, jokes were flying. A couple of them even kept in touch by email.

I also got more involved in my production company. Little by little I produced and directed more than I was in front of the camera. I just got too busy and couldn't do everything.

I then decided to stop working for other productions and only appeared in mine. I figured that people who wanted to see me perform would that way purchase my movies instead of others.

I was pleased about that evolution. Not that I was getting tired of being a porn actress but I always believed my directing and producing would end up being the case after a while.

The job is too intense and too specific. It has to become tiring at some point. Or even worse, it becomes meaningless and boring. As in life, everything can become ordinary when we're doing it out of habit. I saw porn actresses painting their nails during sex scenes, while the cameraman was doing close-ups somewhere else and so you couldn't see her face. It was a scary thought to me. A change before it got to be that way was ideal.

The products I tried to put on the market were personalized. I tried to mix European actresses with Americans, with a more feminine point of view. I believe you can catch a lot of things on camera. One can tell when a girl is pushed to do something she isn't fond of, or work with someone she doesn't like. Just like you can sense a girl that has a real orgasm—she is happy to "work" and really into her scene. Viewers can sense those things if I could sense them.

Being an actress put me closer to the talent than any other director. I just tried to use that privilege to my advantage. At the beginning of the century, talent from Eastern Europe started to visit the US. It gave me the opportunity to film with a specific goal, which was mixing pro-am style with professional quality, favoring the aesthetics instead of the script. By doing this, it allowed me to hire the best-looking performers without having to worry about the language barrier.

It also eased the international sales, without the need to put in annoying dubbing over the action. Dubbing gives me allergic rashes! The lower the budget, the worse the dubbing is. Sometimes it doesn't even match with the actor's mouth movement.

Imagine this in adult movies! One might as well make a comedy! Once, I watched for a whole two minutes, one of my scenes from a US movie that was be sold to France and dubbed by someone else. I never did it again, ever! It was way too embarrassing. Needless to say, people who are aware of my French nationality now think I talk like a duck in agony. It's a weird feeling.

The fact that I didn't have to work anymore for other production companies gave me more freedom as far as where to live, and allowed us to move a little further away from Porn City (Los Angeles). We chose San Francisco!

Chapter 17

LIVING IN THE BAY AREA was fantastic. San Francisco is so refreshing compared to other cities in California. Everything there is so different, including the people. For the most part people there are very opened minded. The people made me feel more comfortable and less worried about been judged regarding my job, on an everyday basis.

We knew someone there from work. Someone we enjoyed being around a lot. His name was Alan. A San Franciscan since childhood, we hung out a lot with him and discovered many great places in the city.

We became friends. Alan was an unusual guy with a lovable personality. Around 50, with sunken, laughing blue eyes, he always seemed to make fun of everyone, just by looking at them. Which was probably the case, knowing his ironic sense of humor.

What amazed me is that he was incapable of seeing the bad in people and never criticized anyone, whatever the circumstances. Alan was also a workaholic. He owned an entire building that he used for work purposes and his apartment was on the top floor. He was his own distributor in his line of work and very successful at it.

He was a heavy marijuana consumer. In fact, we all wondered what kind of drugs he hadn't tried since 1968, as he never left the '70s in his head. We nicknamed him "the Dude" in reference to the movie, *The Big Lebowski*.

Alan's living room was decorated in a unique style. It was filled with flashlights. As you walked in for the first time, you looked at it and wondered if you could bring all your friends and family (perhaps even your family's friends) to his place, in case of a national blackout disaster. I don't know if you've seen anyone with so many flashlights, but I bet not! Sane people can't possibly have that many, especially ugly ones. But to him, all of them were precious, which really made things easy when you're looking for a gift for his birthday.

Professionally he went by the name Duck Dumont. I met him back in L.A. a few years back. He contacted me to perform in one of his movies. His company ("Redboard Video") wasn't producing adult films per se. His line of movies was about Bondage.

For those who aren't too familiar with it, bondage isn't like S&M, it's softer and more psychologically oriented. The best way to describe it would be that bondage is a sexual deviation. It's all about mental and physical humiliation. Mixing bondage and sex was kind of "illegal" for a very long time in the US, and certainly was at that time. The adult industry has the habit of setting its own limits of what you can show to the viewers, convinced that they would get into trouble if they were to show more. So even though it's not a law, they make it their own law and nobody will touch your movie if it doesn't fit the adult industry's own criteria.

As an example, if you were to film a sex scene with a priest and a nun, you were never going to be able to distribute it. The adult industry has already decided that it's not worth the hassle. We already have all the religious groups on our backs, no need to put oil on the fire. It's too bad really - in a case like this one - as it would make a great scene. Apparently, some of these self-inflicted limits have been lifted nowadays.

When Alan called to offer me a part in one of his movies, I was very skeptical regarding my capabilities to perform in such movies. His concept was shooting live scenes, without any interruption, for a whole 20 minutes. It might seem like a small period of time, but it isn't when you don't have a script to follow and zero instructions. I refused to be a submissive; there is always pain involved on top of been humiliated. And even if it's considered "light" pain…well… I really don't enjoy pain! I had to become the dominatrix!

Meaning I would be the leader, the one that controls the entire situation. Which is pretty tough when you don't know anything about the Bondage world!

I went one afternoon to watch and learn on Alan's set. That's when I saw the tools I had to use on another human being, which was known as the "torture kit." The reason I accepted was only because my partner was going to be Kim Wylde, a submissive specialist who did it hundreds of time and "loved" her job.

She told me that, basically, I couldn't hurt her even if I tried. No matter what I did to her, she would enjoy it! What was interesting is that she explained everything I needed to know about all the toys. For example, there is a whipping technique to avoid leaving marks on a person's body.

Also, depending on what material the whip is made of, some make more noise than others when you use them, which makes you look like you're whipping harder than you actually are. I learned about all the tricks, including which candle wax doesn't burn you when it contacts your skin.

Working with her for my first bondage scene reassured me a lot. I don't know how she managed to do it, but somehow she took control of the scene without anyone being able to notice it but Alan and me. I could understand what she wanted me to do, by her eye contact and her attitude, which allowed me to understand her limits. The secret is to start the scene as soft as possible and build up as it goes. The submissive lets the dominant know it is okay to go further, by refusing to do what has been asked of her. A refusal is the ultimate reason for punishment. It becomes your point of reference. On the other hand, if your partner accepts everything right away, and for a long period of time, you know you reached the person's limits of pain. In which case, you need to be really creative to avoid the scene becoming boring, and orient the scene towards more humiliating situations rather than pain. For example, make her lick your shoes or walk her with a dog leash, soft strangulation, light slapping and so on.

The truth? I loved it! I seriously doubted that I would before actually doing it.

It is strange how we can discover things about ourselves sometimes. Anyhow, at the end of the scene, guilt took over. I guess I might have felt bad about enjoying it so much. I got laughed at in return. Kim begged me to stop asking her how she was doing and called ME "crazy" for worrying! She said it was great and hoped we would be working together again very soon. She was hyper and giggling—she looked like a human-size battery just re-charged. I was a little confused. It seemed like I had just given her a nice massage!

I ended up working for Alan regularly, as he was coming to L.A. every two months or so. I soon even made a reputation for myself as being violent with words and attitude. Some actors told me my facial expression would change dramatically as soon as I heard the word "action," and I looked scary, as if I was ready to kill someone! They didn't recognize the sweet Rebecca anymore!

I got better at it each time, and Alan set me up with newcomers pretty fast. Being new at it and taking the submissive part was risky! I felt the need to spend time with them beforehand, to test the toys and have a real conversation about the whole thing. My biggest fear was to hurt someone, which would not be the case if they were into it. What I learned was that a real submissive feels pleasure by being mistreated.

One of the parts I liked the most was the way Alan filmed it. Live, with no cuts. He said that it is the only way to do it. It looks real, because it simply was. Its technique gave me the pressure of concentrating on my partner every second and pushed me to think fast, with imagination, according to my partner's reactions, because I had to create a stage instantly.

It had to look real and natural, with a lot of intensity. Hesitating would ruin my credibility and the scene would then be ruined as well.

So that's how I made people jump into garbage, crawl naked in the mud, eat dog food while barking, climb into a tree imitating a monkey, or drink water out of the toilet... Fun times! The only time I may have run out of ideas was how to end the scene, to make an exit. I could see Alan in the corner of my eye, laughing, without ever helping me! My favorite ending, that could also be adapted to almost any situation created, was to tie up and gag my partner, explaining out loud that I was leaving him and would come back in a few hours, if he behaved enough.

Of course, there was a "safe word" to use for the submissive if something went wrong, if he/she couldn't take it anymore, which would make everyone stop right away. Complaints, whining, yelling or even crying wasn't a sign of anything to Alan. Some people can literally enjoy it and exteriorize their emotions that way.

The safe word was "stop everything." Pretty explicit, you would say. That's what I thought too, until Michael J .Cox, an adult performer, decided to try bondage for the first time.

We knew each other pretty well, since we worked many times together and went along fine. I still can't believe what happened that day. For some reason, Michael couldn't remember the safe word! Not only did he forget, but also the panic made him freeze completely. Taking his negative attitude for a sign of provocation ("I'm fine, hit me harder!") I increased the intensity gradually and humiliated him properly as well. Of course, I heard him complaining several times, but couldn't understand what he was saying, since he was stammering with fear. When I think about it today, I believe I really scared the living daylights out of him!

I know it is easy for me to say this, since I was always the dominatrix, but bondage is a game, where we all play a role. Poor Michael. He kept freezing on every opportunity that I made and I kept roughing him up, threatening to punish him harder if he didn't keep quiet!! He was red and furious.

A few minutes before the end, I remember noticing something was odd. Perhaps it was the look on his face? I couldn't see it sooner, since I had been ordering him to look at the floor for so long, which made me slow down a little. How awful I felt when I realized what had happened! I apologized a hundred times, but somehow never felt it was enough. There is nothing more frustrating that not being able to undo an honest mistake.

That night, I wouldn't let it go and kept harassing him on the phone to make sure he was "okay." I can't be sure, but Michael may have said he was fine and that there was no need to apologize, just so he could finally go to bed. The funny thing is, I don't know which of the two of us was more ashamed.

Moving to San Francisco and becoming Alan's neighbor allowed us to work together more often. As the opportunity presented itself, we shortly developed a new line for Redboard Video, called "Torment," which turned out to be very successful among bondage movies.

"The Dude" passed away from following a "no carb diet" which lead to a heart attack in 2006. I still miss him dearly. Since then, I have a serious heinous feeling towards any diet rules. Happily I'm lucky enough so far, for not having weight issues, because I can assure you: I would remain fat until my last breath.

Around this time award winning photographer Larry Sultan asked to come to my place during a production. Unfamiliar with the adult industry, Larry was working on his latest book called *The Valley*. What he was hoping for, by being there, was to capture the atmosphere and facial expressions. He meant to discover something more interesting than the obvious. Larry Sultan was the most discreet photographer I ever met. You easily could forget he was there taking photos.

I was excited by his presence and couldn't wait to see the results. I was expecting artistic pictures of my house, someone's eyes looking at the horizon filled with emotion, a hand on someone's shoulder, or simply something that nobody ever caught but him being there.

What in fact came of it that day was mainly my dogs. My four hairy babies inspired him more than hanging around naked people at work! Larry couldn't have made me happier and more proud. The picture he used was the four of them, bending (magically at the same exact time, for a fraction of second) as I passed by. Mr. Sultan was published widely and that's how my boxers ended up in the *New York Times*.

It turns out that his project was exhibited all over the world in various museums, like the Guggenheim Museum in NYC, San Francisco Museum of Modern Art, Los Angeles County Museum of Art, then in Italy, Switzerland, France, London and Belgium.

Having my boxers worldly exposed, and still are as of today (since my last interview about that precise picture was for an exhibitor in Miami only 2 years ago), is special. In a way that it makes them immortals.

More than once, I was so tempted to go to those exhibits and just stand there next to my dogs' picture. To hear what people might think of it, but also to approach anyone slightly interested in it. I would have said something like, "Those are mine, I have proof!"

There is an expression in French: *pèter son soutif*. The raw translation of it, is, "To blow up your bra," which means you are so proud, your chest inflates up to the point where your bra cracks. That's how I felt. Only, unfortunately, my boobs never got bigger. Speaking of expressions, they don't travel very well from one country to another. As you learn a new language, you're often tempted to translate everything word by word, which isn't always a good idea. You should see people's faces when, in a competitive situation you say, with attitude, "Pfffffffffff, finger in the nose!" (Instead of "A walk in the park," in the US.) Or when you're desperately trying to go to bed and finally make an exit, saying to everyone, "Okay, well, I am going to put the meat in the sheets!" (Going to bed)! Not only are your guests now being disgusted by your hygiene, they are also expecting you to come back!

Chapter 18

WHEN PEOPLE WANT to get in the adult industry, the first place they contact, beside agents, is adult companies. The fact that I had a website and also a fan club made it easy to reach me. My inbox was full of guys, so when a girl wrote I tended to notice. Needless to say, being on the road for publicity purposes or a dancing tour made the whole thing a little easier for helping girls get in the business.

I decided to help on three different occasions. The first girl was a stripper from Anchorage, Alaska called Erin. I met her during a Spice Network event in the strip club she was working at. She asked me to help her to become an adult actress, saying she couldn't stand doing her job anymore and needed badly to get out of Alaska. I then arranged her travel accommodations to California and filmed her first scene. She was what we called a "natural." She seemed to have done it all her life and nothing indimidated her. There was a certain responsibility I had, to bring a civilian into our world. The minimum I could do was to explain in detail how things worked, along with giving good referrals (starting with friends) and a black list of who she should avoid working for. But "kids" remain kids, and advice is often made not to follow.

The perfect example to illustrate this was Bobbi Barrington. She was a very cute blonde from Perth, Australia. She had been insisting for weeks by email that she wanted to work with me, and she finally flew to come work for my production. She was anxious and apprehensive of our industry and what could happen, so she stayed at our house in San Francisco for several days before heading to L.A.

The three of us took the time to make sure she understood everything, and we even booked work for her in advance so she would start with trustable people (friends, like Ron and Nic, for example).

What she did once she got there was the exact opposite. Bobbi was a strange girl. I never truly understood why she wanted to do adult movies. She was full of negative thoughts towards our industry to begin with.

From what I heard, she purposely created negative situations, like offering sex to people to be hired. Unfortunately, having such an attitude can only attract people that will abuse you. She ended up flying back to Perth a few months later.

My third experience couldn't have gone any better. If you have been paying attention throughout this book you probably realize by now that I am being sarcastic.

She was also from Alaska, but we had never met before. I'm not trying to hide her identity. I just can't remember her name! Let's call her "V." She contacted me through my website and seemed to be extremely motivated. The San Francisco airport was far away from where we lived, so "V" agreed that I would pick her up at the shuttle station instead. When I got there, the bus she was on was full. With a warm welcoming smile on my face, I watched every single person getting off of it. Once or twice I thought I recognized her, and waved at the wrong person. Soon the vehicle was empty. "V" wasn't on it.

Assuming she missed her shuttle, I left her a message on her cell phone and simply waited for the next one that came half an hour later. Only the same thing happened! And then, an hour later, still nothing. I kept calling her, but the phone was going straight to voicemail.

What bothered me the most was that she couldn't have missed her flight since she called me from the airport, saying she was boarding. Could she have taken the wrong shuttle? Why wasn't she answering her phone? Why wasn't she calling me? Worried but powerless, I left the airport and went home to check my email. I didn't have any messages from her. I called her house in Alaska and spoke to her boyfriend. He had been with her at the airport and saw "V" getting on the plane. I then called the airline right away and explained the situation, but no one had the authority to reveal passenger's information, which was predictable.

The whole thing started to seriously stink. Philippe and I came back to the terminal to check one more time and drove around, stopping at bars nearby, until nightfall. But still no trace of her. Nothing. "V" had vanished! Nothing we could think of was reassuring. We also felt responsible for her, since we were the ones bringing her over. The worst-case scenario came to our minds and we gradually were overcome with panic.

A cute young girl from a small town, disappearing in California, as she was travelling alone! I know we saw too many movies, but thousands of people vanish every year in the US, and that is a fact, not fiction.

From that point on, only one thing was left to do: go to the police and tell everything. Rick joined us to add his name to the statement as well, hoping the greater our number, the more persuasive we would be.

The guys at the police station seemed to have taken us seriously and promised to inform us about the evolution of their investigation. Which they did, as they nicely called us one hour later, to confirm that the vanished girl did get on the flight and even took her checked luggage after her plane landed. There was no doubt now that she was in California.

Anxiously, the three of us stayed silent all night. Hours seemed to last forever. Waiting was real torture. I kept imagining her, laying on the side of the road somewhere. At 1 a.m., the police called again. They had found her! Alive and well, she was comfortably at home in Alaska!

I was shocked and confused. I couldn't even speak. The police were empathetic and said she should call in a couple of minutes to explain and apologize, as they had firmly suggested she do that. She almost did, but it was her boyfriend I talked to instead.

I couldn't believe my ears. "V" had made it all the way to the terminal where I was expecting her, and got out of the shuttle and saw me (I know she did because he even described the way I was dressed). Then, she instantly changed her mind about doing movies and decided to hide from me before taking the next bus back to the airport, turning her phone off while she was at it. I remember asking why didn't she say anything—if not in person, at least over the phone or by email. "She was afraid," he said. Somehow I felt like a 7 foot, 300 pound scary guy with a hood, wearing heavy skull rings on my fingers! We were a few feet away from each other and she hid? Just like that, after several weeks of email and phone exchanges, not to mention the half a day of travel to come to San Francisco! Which planet exactly was she from?

"Vanished V" unfairly made the other girls pay for her silliness, because since that day, I never again helped another girl get into the adult industry.

Chapter 19

ONE DAY I WAS WALKING around in the Castro area of San Francisco when two guys came up to me asking if I was French. Amused by their approach, I let them engage in further conversation. Even more amusing, they wanted me to go to a casting call the next day for a movie they were working on, one of them being an indie director. Yeah, right!

There is no need to argue in that case—the best way to get rid of people is to agree with them so you can get on with your life. So I did, after taking their business card along with me. Let's face it, being recruited in the street for a movie just never happens.

They were either fakes or non-professionals who were trying to make a porn movie. Either way, they evidently knew who I was, because knowing my nationality and having a "camera involved somewhere" didn't require a diploma from Harvard to figure out what was happening.

I'm not paranoid or self-centered. I only learned by experience that the obvious is never written on people's faces. Especially in my line of work.

Oh, and I forgot to mention a tiny detail—an adult shop had the idea to put up a huge Rebecca Lord billboard in front of their store, on the sidewalk of Van Ness Avenue (which is one of the main streets in San Francisco), nicely lit at night by three different colored spotlights.

Did I ever abuse this notoriety in my everyday life? Yes, tremendously. The cashier at Ralphs was letting me use the handicap cart, late at night, to drive around in the store's alley. I know, it is not as impressive as if I had driven a police car with the siren and lights on during rush hour so all the cars in front of you move away like their lives depend on it. But, I never dared to ask. Like my friend Nic always says: "No guts, no glory." My friends are born poets. What can I say. Now, perhaps after this book sees the light of day and magically reaches the hand of someone nice enough…

Anyway, once home, I decided to Google the name on the business card, just out of curiosity. I was surprised to then discover that Caveh Zahedi really was an independent film director!

Motivated by curiosity more than ever, I went to the appointment the next day. After all, the project might be real and they simply might need a porn actress to play a part, which isn't uncommon. When they explained what the movie was all about, everything made sense. The film happened to be a comedy, about sex addiction! My character would be the main actor's wife, a 25 to 30-year-old French girl, puritan and repressed. What a perfect idea to have an adult actress play that part. It makes the whole thing even funnier!

Having said that, neither the director nor the cameraman mentioned anything about it. Hypocritically enough, they even asked me what I was doing for a living. What a joke. They had enough courage to recruit me in the street, but not enough to take responsibility for their knowledge?

Fine, I was not going to give them the satisfaction of helping them out. Let's see how long it will take them to spit it out. I was actually amused by it. After a few dialogue tests, they even pushed it by asking me to fake an orgasm! That took the cake! Then I got hired.

The first days of shooting were interesting. I didn't know we would spend hours just to shoot a couple lines of dialogue to get it the way the director wanted. I enjoyed doing it too because the story had a message to pass on, something to say. Fred, the cameraman, kept telling me how impressed he was by my lack of shyness in front of the camera. That he had never seen a novice as comfortable as me before. At first, I thought he was still challenging me to ease their guilty conscience, but after a while, I got to know them better and started to doubt my assumptions. I kept rejecting the idea of such a misunderstanding, until their attitude was just too obvious. They really didn't know.

What have I done? They will find out somehow, it was only a matter of time! I was so embarrassed! I looked like a big fat liar, that's what I looked like. In another situation, it would not have mattered so much, but we were shooting a mainstream movie, financed by different investors.

My image would have consequences, plain and simple. I needed to tell them now. Then it occurred to me that it was too late. Everyone involved in this project worked for two weeks already. I'm not even mentioning what a 15 day budget represented for an independent film, possibly almost half of it? All of it couldn't possibly be thrown in the trash! I also selfishly feared that the movie would not be finished. They could replace me, which meant I would have worked for nothing. I was cornered.

I then decided to keep playing my part, hoping I was worrying for nothing. Until one day, the movie had to be suspended for financial reasons. They had to edit the rush of what had been shot so far to show the investors the first half, so they would agree to finance the rest of it. Several months later, I received a phone call. Caveh had just shown what we did to his investors. Cold as ice, he asked for us to meet.

He knew. Everyone knew. Right after the private showing, people went up to him. It was over.

I remember Caveh mentioning to me words like "shocked," "humiliated," or even "betrayed." I liked the guy, he was an unusual and moving person. I felt ashamed. For the first time I even felt bad about me being titled a "Porn Star," like it was filthy or unhealthy. What I expected and feared happened: the movie was suspended.

A few months later, they contacted me again. Some investors had an epiphany. They realized they could use my name and the irony of the situation to their advantage. The exact same reason that created the confusion a year before pushed them to finally finance the rest of what was needed for Caveh.

The director added a few things to his script, some kind of "voice over" with images of me saying I was a make-up artist, justifying that they didn't know who I really was. Which made them look like victims, just in case.

After all that time, it was a happy ending. On the other hand, the mood during the shoot was never the same afterwards. I believe they were looking at me in a new light. They never got over it. I wasn't the sweet girl anymore, I was a question mark—a pervert or a victim? Apparently, I couldn't possibly be anything else. They finally opted for the victim; the last day of shooting, some members of the crew nicely offered to help me.

Sincere and delicate, they talked to me about some associations they knew about. Which I honestly appreciated, but of course, declined the offer.

I then became an even bigger question mark to them! They couldn't understand. They couldn't figure out why I seemed so comfortable and happy the way I was. Needless to say they aren't alone. It is a typical, worldwide reaction.

Here is another irony: I don't judge any of them. So, as usual, I didn't feel like explaining myself to Caveh and his friends. The truth is, I don't have to, and for a very simple reason. I have nothing to feel guilty about.

The movie, *I Am a Sex Addict*, was well received and even nominated for awards in various independent film festivals.

Chapter 20

For us, producing movies from San Francisco, with talent, crew and equipment being in L.A., wasn't an easy thing to do. We were just too far away from the industry and too much time was wasted flying back and forth to L.A.

Neither Philippe nor I were motivated to move back to the Valley and were seeking an alternate place to live. That's when we thought of Las Vegas. Only a 3 hour drive from L.A. or half hour of flight time. It was perfect! At the time, a few people from the adult industry already lived there, like the sweet Ana Malle.

Sadly, Rick wouldn't follow us this time. Our adoptive son was called back to L.A. for an attractive job proposal. Plus, I secretly suspect he was tired of moving from place to place almost every year! Bottom line, and after several hesitations, we agreed that we must cut the umbilical cord and let him go! Not too far away from us, though.

For those of you who have been to Vegas, our house was a couple blocks away from the Rio Casino and the Palms, facing the desert. I truly loved every single day living there. What does that city have to offer beside its gambling and its partying nightlife? Everything that another "normal" city can have, but 24 hours a day, since lots of people in this town work nights. You want to go to the dry cleaners or the post office at 1 o'clock in the morning? No problem. If you hurt yourself on the way back, make sure you stop at the pharmacy, too. Also the indescribable Nevada desert. Yes, Las Vegas doesn't have an architectural style, or a "soul" like New York City or San Francisco, but frankly who cares when you have such natural beauty surrounding it! I never had the same view from my living room window—the sunlight and clouds changed everything every day. The desert seems endless. It is so peaceful and resourceful that I enjoyed losing myself there. Perhaps the same way some people can relate to the ocean, or snow-covered mountains.

Las Vegas is also the only city where a boat actually hit my front door, tearing down the wall around it. I couldn't be mad at the boat owner—the pictures that came out of it were too good! Picture it in a magazine: "Boat hits porn star's front yard in the middle of the desert!" It does take several seconds before your brain realizes what happened. The house was downhill, and the boat being up hill, the trailer hitch simply broke off. After that, it's just a matter of being in its way or not. It's mathematical.

Contrary to what you might think, being in the desert, many residents owned boats in this area. Lake Mead is only a few miles away. Around 120 miles long, it's a huge lake that has many beautiful places to discover, which I gratefully used for shooting purposes several times.

The warm weather allowed me to shoot movies outside more often than in San Francisco, mostly all year long. Rare was the time where I had to rent a house or a place to shoot sex scenes, even in L.A. I always favored the outdoors because I believe natural light is prettier and makes better images. I also believe "the outdoors" has always been most people's fantasy, as long as it's not always the same location seen in zillions of movies and has great backgrounds. A big plus was finding an unusual concept and an extraordinary place. Which involves a minimum of scouting. An adult film doesn't have the same budget that a mainstream movie has and "scouting" is usually not part of it. You can't just hire a professional to do it, you have to do it yourself, and it comes out of your own pocket!

Since the scenes involve naked people, outdoor places have to be isolated. It really wasn't that complicated, it just required more imagination and perseverance. What complicated things were indoor places. Owners gladly rented their places to shoot a film, but an adult film? Less likely! It just reduces your choices dramatically.

I love scouting. How rewarding to find a magic place after seeking it all day! It allows you to discover many areas you would have never seen otherwise too, mainly because you have to do off roads. I enjoyed finding an old abandoned ranch, hills with breathtaking views, ruins, or an isolated, magical area in the desert.

One took me a couple of days to find. The Nevada desert always has a farm or a route somewhere and since it's flat, people can see you from far away. But it was worth looking for. The place was unique and impossible to be seen from miles away. The sand was so dry, it was hard and cracked for miles, surrounded by hills on the horizon. I found out, a couple years later, that I wasn't the only one to have discovered the place. It's been used for a few TV commercials and in a couple of movies, too.

    As for us, we challenged ourselves to use it in the most creative way possible a sex scene can allow. We placed a modern red sofa in the middle of it, with a green coffee table next to it. To increase the contrast we were looking for, we put a round fish tank with two goldfish in it. We called our little friends Dudulle One, and his identical twin, Dudulle Two. Friendly and very quiet, our guests made the whole difference to the picture. Of course, having a sexy bride wearing a wedding dress, with her groom in a tuxedo (myself) next to it, did bring out the best in them.

    As I was too busy to pay attention to the Dudulle brothers, it took me a while before I realized that sadly they had died before we even started to shoot. Their stomachs up in the air, the fish tank's water was almost boiling. I guess we didn't think ahead that the end of July in the desert couldn't benefit their health positively.

    But let's not revive sad memories. I only wish to add this. It secretly brings me satisfaction, imagining that one day, someone from one of the big budget TV commercials (copycat thieves!) must have run into two fish skeletons in the middle of the desert and must have literally flipped out!

    Living in Las Vegas attracts friends to come visit like magnets. As soon as we moved in, we suddenly felt needed and missed like never before by friends from overseas, but also from the US.

    Since most of my American friends were living three hours away, our weekends were quite busy. As time passed, I found out as well that a few adult actresses were living in the same city as us, for various reasons. It increased motivation for some of my friends since they could combine work and gambling in the same weekend.

    Sin City is a Disneyland for adults, and as such, Vegas offers many fun options as far as places for productions. Themed motels is one of them. Created for couples that come to the city to get married in an hour, sometimes even to get married by a priest disguised as Elvis Presley, those unique places just followed the same spirit.

    Of course, it isn't as fancy as the hotels and casinos, but shooting adult films requires a lot of discretion. I can't picture a crew passing through the casino floor of a hotel with lightning equipment and cameras without getting attention from security.

    I mean, you can always do it with small equipment that you may hide in bags, for a small budget movie, but since you can't film the hotel itself or the casino, it becomes meaningless to go there and take the risk to get caught. Once you get to the room, it's just another room with a bed, and could be anywhere!

The advantage of a motel is that you can come and go as you please without being noticed, since the room's front door opens on the outside. Themed motels were nothing but small versions of studios built for adult movies—the Disco bedroom, the Barbie Suite, the Gangster bedroom, the Egyptian, the lunar moon landing (the bed being a space capsule), and so on. As far as I'm concerned, the Dracula's castle won my heart.

By the way, if anyone goes there and notices the headboard which looks like a headstone being broken, think of me.

Chapter 21

TIME PASSES TOO FAST SOMETIMES. I realized I hadn't come home to visit my birth country as often as I should. In 11 years, I only went twice! I guess I didn't miss it that much because I was happy where I was, and luckily my family and friends made the trip to come to the US.

Having your loved ones over is great, but still, it isn't the same thing. So Philippe and I decided to combine some private time in France with a little bit of business, as we wanted to attend an adult convention in Barcelona, Spain.

Most professionals going to European conventions are usually there to get new contacts/relationships with European productions for foreign sales purposes. It also allows you to understand better what works there and what doesn't.

It felt very strange being in a convention where I barely knew anybody. Other than familiar faces like Ron Jeremy, Rocco Siffredi or Silvia Saint, the only few times I recognized a face, I acted like that person was a missed friend I hadn't seen for a while! I was happy to see Pierre Woodman there, who introduced us to his brother Vincent who had recently moved to Barcelona. Pierre had produced his own internet-platform, which in 2005 was uncommon in the adult industry, especially in Europe, where internet porn (VOD) was at its early stage.

Unexpectedly, attending this event took my life and career in an unexpected new direction. An appealing two-year contract deal was offered to me, as a director, from a Spanish company called "IFG."

The offer needed an immediate decision. Being rushed sometimes feels awkward at first, like when someone holds the door for you, but you're too far away and have to run. Since I can't stand missing good opportunities, we decided to stay there, for a 2 year period! Things in life are often simpler than we like to think. Rick flew to bring us our dogs and we moved to a beautiful furnished house near Barcelona. It was lovely and interesting to have my American friends, like Rick or Ron, coming to visit in Europe, making them discover things, somehow the same way they did for us in the United States.

A shocking feeling was to see how small the cars were in Europe! Wait…I think I had the same feeling years back about how big things were the day I landed in the US!

It's amazing how you can get used to things after so many years. Things and lifestyles too. Like expecting to have a refilled Coca Cola or ice tea. I witnessed some American colleagues that had a business meeting at a bar in a fancy hotel for several hours and had to dispute their $200 bill for just sodas!

To embark on a production in Europe meant finding a new faithful and professional crew that I could trust. Which wasn't easy when you were gone for so long. I realized I simply didn't know anyone.

That's when I thought of David for the camera, the French director/cameraman from my early years. I hoped he knew enough equipped people too, beside photographers. As far as editing, I gladly didn't need anybody at this point. We already had enough practice, having invested in our own equipment and doing it ourselves.

What I needed badly was to get back into the game of knowing which actors and actresses are out there or not. I understood quickly that things in Europe had changed dramatically. 80% of female performers were now from Eastern Europe, like Hungary, Czech Republic and Russia. None of those girls worked freelance, all of them had an agent out there.

It's a strange thing at first—you can never talk to them directly by phone or email, like I used to do in the US, even for a casting. It somehow always made me doubt that the girls were the ones deciding about the scenes, or if the agent was. Unfortunately, being against that practice didn't change the fact that no other choices were left for me. Surprisingly too, some girls were officially on different agents' websites, each of them announcing those girls as exclusives. I soon understood agents were negotiating the girls between them, as if they were objects, which seems to me very petty (not to say pimpy) of them. And lastly, I had to find out locations of where to shoot. The choice was large since I could shoot wherever I wanted to, all over Europe. You would certainly think that being French would help a lot. It's seems entirely logical, only I knew more about the United States than European countries, where I had simply never set foot before (except for France). I had to put on my scouting hat again, and travel all over!

I first went to Prague for a week. I thought since most of the talent was there, might as well see what the city had to offer and get closer to the performers, if possible. A lot of things there were in fact more practical and affordable than Spain or France, like equipped studios, villas, stores to rent, trains and so on. Life in general was cheaper and Prague was offering great opportunities for any filmmakers.

I also went looking for outdoor locations in warmer countries. It could be France, Spain or Italy. Beautiful as those places could be, it is very difficult to find an uninhabited spot, unlike in the United States. The bigger the country is, the more it offers sites with no one around for miles. I often get asked, "Does size really matter?" I agree, it does! We are just not talking about the same thing!!!

Scouting the Canary Islands was another memorable moment. At the rental car place they had no automatic cars! Every vehicle on the island had shifts. And it's not like they would generously fly an automatic car over just because I explained I got my driver's license in the US and could only drive automatics!

My days there ended up being ridiculous. I thought I would never come back alive. Tenerife has 10% flat ground and 90% hills since, as we all know (right?), it's a mountainous and volcanic place. My left foot was so tense that I managed to break my heel in the car. People passing by were screaming at me, which was normal, but the weirdest thing is that they were doing it in German. I thought it was very odd for a Spanish Island. Eventually, not that strange when I found out that the majority of the population there is German. I just wished I had known it beforehand. I would have traded in my Spanish dictionary for a German one! As for finding someone speaking English, the airport seemed to have been holding the only ones hostage.

All this trouble would finally wind up, for the first movie, in one of the Balearic Islands. In Majorca. It was wintertime, and I chose to postpone my other projects in Prague for later during the year.

I rented a Villa far away from any town, in the middle of the countryside, to benefit from the outdoor area, which was big enough to accommodate everybody involved in the project. Shooting in Europe needed a very different type of organization, since I had people coming from all over the place. France, Spain, Hungary and Czech Republic.

Life is full of unexpected surprises. It snowed there the entire time. Majorca hasn't had snow in March for the last 70 years! That's how lucky I am. Someday, I will live in Theory, because in Theory, everything is always fine.

Anyway, that said, the Villa became the only place left to film, which wasn't too practical with everyone staying there and having nowhere else to go. The surface of the rooms appeared smaller in reality than in the agency pictures. But even with uncomfortable accommodations, the crew and talent got along very well and we managed to live and work in harmony.

Although one girl gave me a hard time right away. Her pretext was that her bedroom was too small and too noisy. Because of it, she demanded financial compensation and threatened to leave. I personally call it unreasonable blackmail. I guess it all depends where you stand. Unfortunately for me, she was the leader of the four girls. When she realized her demands weren't going to go through, she started to manipulate the others, which left all of them in a constant bad mood.

Ignoring this situation would have been like having employees gradually going on strike. From what I understood, the blackmailer thought we were such a long way from anything, it would have complicated the possibilities to replace her. She was wrong. I fired her in a heartbeat and found another actress in 24 hours. Everything went smoothly after that.

This situation bugged me for a while, more than it should have. That kind of behavior was unusual to me, as I never witnessed anything like it before, during my whole career in the US. Was it my fault? Of course, it could have been, only I can objectively say that I was fair, respectful, and even friendlier than most porn directors.

As my European experience increased, I happened to be confronted in similar situations, which brought me to the conclusion that even if talent from all over the world remains the same, there is a cultural difference that needed to be taken into account. Most Eastern Europe actresses have a hard time associating authority with kindness. In other words, being nice is perceived as a weakness, and they don't respect you anymore. If you are nice, you are stupid. That's what they think of you.

There is also another factor, the fact that a porn star's career in Europe is very short because of way less work opportunities, and changing mentalities. Actresses don't see their jobs as a career with a future, they can only see it in the present. They just think about making money today, never thinking about making it tomorrow. It makes the whole concept a total different one than in America, for instance, where a porn actress would not dare to blackmail a producer for any reason. She would be too afraid of damaging her career and ruining her reputation.

Since I am philosophizing poorly about female performers, it might seem fair to speculate about male performers as well, since theirs was also a different attitude I wasn't use to. As nice and professional some of them could be doesn't excuse their obvious macho state of mind. Some are better than others, but overall it just shows, especially in Latin countries. There is no doubt about it being a cultural thing.

To be more specific, it has nothing to do with the sexual intercourse itself, but about the attitude towards it and its approach. Already in pre-production, I found myself struggling to talk to them over the phone about their work, or even about their wardrobe. They sometimes asked to talk to my husband! Amused by it, Philippe gladly played the role, as I was boiling next to him, using sign language.

As expected, the same ones weren't any better on the set. They would naturally come to Philippe to ask questions, even though he was officially the production photographer. Frankly, it surprised me more than it bothered me, and fighting this was, and still is, useless. My priorities remain the movies, which require the talent to feel comfortable. If I have to go through this to obtain the results I need, then so be it. That's how I started to use my understanding husband in those awkward situations, to get what I needed.

Shooting in Europe wasn't worse or better than shooting in the US, once you adapt. It was just different. One of the plus sides was the feeling of being in a summer camp on every project. Plus, being stuck for a week or more with the crew gave me the opportunity to know them more personally, which (most of the time) brought us closer to each other.

The other plus side was the challenge—it is tougher to shoot an adult movie in Europe of the same quality than in the US, especially with an equal budget. There is a language barrier, having to bring people together from all over the place; and simply just being too far away from L.A., with all its technical advantages.

Tougher means more work and longer days for everyone, even for visitors. Three Italian journalists from the RAI (which is a public TV network in Italy) were making a documentary about my being a female director in the adult industry, and had to follow us all week long. They were so motivated and enthusiastic about every little detail that seemed so ordinary to us that they actually looked like aliens to everyone. Their friendly and respectful attitude blended perfectly with the crew, only they hammered us with giveaway questions like, "So, you guys actually eat together?" They were constantly interrupting us for anything with their camera in our faces. We quickly decided to give them different call times rather than the official ones so we could have our early meetings peacefully. It became a joke, and some people were even hiding from them at times.

I know, that was mean (but it was funny!). My point being how exhausted our documentary friends were, after only a couple of days.

They weren't familiar with such long days, and they had a hard time keeping up with us. It wouldn't have been that amusing if they hadn't made such an effort to hide it, like showing up late with their hair messed up, sticky eyes and out of breath, announcing they woke up early, but would gladly take another cup of coffee. It reminded me of my grandmother who proudly always announced every morning how little she slept all night, forgetting that she snored so loud, the trembling walls still remembering it.

A year in Spain had gone by, and I didn't miss not working at all in front of the camera. Without ever reaching the point where I needed to sit down and think about it, my full reconversion happened naturally. I was now over 30 years old and it felt logical that young actresses and new faces in this business should take over.

Unfortunately, my contract with IFG ended earlier than scheduled. They just couldn't pay me anymore! The company was as dry as the fish's skeleton left in Nevada.

Knowing before hiring me that they couldn't follow up financially, they looked at the whole picture, but several movies weren't enough to save the company in such a short period of time.

The honest way would have been to warn me when we signed the agreement, so we could have weighed up the risks. But by being too proud, they didn't. Too bad. I would have been open to compromises. Instead, I found out during a pre-production, which made me spend my own money for 2/3 of the project.

Here we go again for another breach of contract! Fire in the hole! I then turned to my friend Pierre Woodman who knew everyone and everything in Europe, and he sent me to his "Private" general manager Javier (they have their office around Barcelona). He suggested that we should hire his own lawyer. The lawyer resolved the problem to my advantage pretty swiftly and we were out of Spain for good.

Shortly after that disappointing event, we took some time off, and treated each other to a long vacation in Brazil. We hadn't had a vacation for more than 12 years. Samba!

Chapter 22

WE EXPERIENCED BRAZIL to the fullest. Rio de Janeiro, Buzios, Cabo Frio, Euro Preto, Belo Horizonte! Jumping from one city to another, we were lapping up everything we saw.

This colorful country gives such a change of scenery! Brazilians are unique in the way they welcome tourists. Nothing compares to their infectious joy. You can't teach people that kind of talent; it is in them. When you first witness it and then share it with them, it is addictive. Everywhere else seems oddly insipid.

Completely under the spell of the moment, take a wild guess of what happened next? That's right, we decided to move there. A few unavoidable administrative procedures later, and we were settled in.

Producing movies there wasn't an option. As surprising as it might seem, Brazil isn't suitable for it. That's the reason why there aren't any real international Brazilian porn productions. I will spare you any analysis on Brazil's mentality, but filming sex just isn't their culture. It has nothing to do with Puritanism; it's really about being exposed. Sex is very present in Brazilian society. It's a natural thing. Nudity is never a problem and there is very little censorship.

Unlike the US, the God-fearing people do not interfere on sex matters. They don't need to. You can have plenty of sex with lots of people but if they see a camera, they run away and go back to playing soccer on the next beach!

So for us, since a new adventure was presenting itself, why not try something entirely different for a while? The adult industry can wait a little, we'll see how things turns out. We hadn't had a vacation in such long time!

We quickly had the idea of opening a restaurant. Either that or getting into the moving business, since we had plenty experience. To differentiate ourselves from any other Brazilian moving company, we would bring croissants with moving boxes or something like that! Just kidding. I got you here, didn't I?

Anyway, we found a great spot and managed to restore a restaurant and nightclub in Belo Horizonte, Minas Gerais. Although Rio de Janeiro is a much more attractive city, the tremendous difference between the social classes (rich/poor) makes the city a dangerous place to live freely. Unlike Belo Horizonte, where an existing middle class establishes an economical balance.

It became urgent for me to learn Portuguese. Unlike my experience in the US where I had the luxury to learn English as life went by, this time I needed to understand my employees and clients right away. Laughing with them when I sensed it was the appropriate behavior wasn't enough.

I then took Portuguese classes with a University's English teacher. At the same time, I took bartending classes as well, since I wanted to be directly involved in the nightclub. I found myself really enjoying it, and even specialized in *flair* bartending. Yes, guys, like in the movie *Coyote Ugly*!

I wish I could tell you some great stories about me jumping around the bar, playing with three or four bottles at once, while my 50 (or more) most faithful customers were shouting with joy and cheering for more. But I can't.

The truth is, the place just never had the chance to make it that far. I am seriously thinking about writing another book about my experiences in Brazil, but just in case I don't, let me give you one juicy example (out of many) that could vaguely explain the failure.

Before the grand opening, we advertised the place like crazy for months and plastered the whole city. In the advertisement I made, I couldn't stress enough the importance of having an "American Bar" in that area of the city. There were none at the time.

We even put up a huge billboard in front of our building during the entire time of the renovation. I am proud to say it was a great move commercially speaking.

We were very proud, until we found out afterwards that "American Bar" is actually used in Brazil for "whore house." Whore houses being legal there. Of course nobody told me about it.

But I assure you, it is called American Bar, and it is pointless to ask why. I can hear puritans and conservatives rolling on the floor laughing as they are reading this. What a perfect irony—a porn star trying to open a restaurant got it wrong, and was in fact declaring the Grand Opening of a whore house instead! It serves her right! (Except maybe for Sarah Palin. To be understood, irony requires a minimum of subtlety).

Oh, we got people coming in all right, and do I need to mention 100% of them were single guys? But they left right away, as if my place smelled like decomposing rats. They must have thought, "Where are the girls???!"

Chapter 23

A THREE-YEAR BREAK from my "normal" life was about to end. As soon as I stepped foot out of Brazil, I got back into the swing of things. I almost immediately got an offer to direct a movie for Video Marc Dorcel, a prestigious French XXX production company.

Ten scripts later, one got finally approved. And then, since it became officially their script, they decided to change everything from A to Z, to more reflect a Dorcel product. I didn't quite understand the point of hiring me for what I made in the past and that they liked, if it was to direct a formatted product I barely had a saying in doing.

As I recall, they asked me to join the team to bring my footprint in. Why cut me off from making decisions then? I could barely choose the cast. I had to hire some actress I didn't want, plus they choose the talent's clothing, locations, and worst, the way I could shoot a sex scene. Might as well give the movie to any subordinate already working for them. They didn't need me for that.

Go figure what they were thinking. I hated working that way, especially when I constantly had to justify my every move to someone. I surely wasn't used to it!

As soon as an American company chooses to sign you up, for whatever reason it might be, they trust you to give the expected result. If they feel like you aren't capable of it, they just don't hire you. If the result proves them wrong, they take responsibility for it and you are toast in the future. Frankly? It makes perfect sense. But then again, my logic has been highly influenced by the "American way."

Anyway, the script was original, with a brand new concept: secretaries! It's amazing how many secretaries can be horny nowadays. Yes, France is avid for novelties. Although the title was a small give away (*Secretaries*), it truly aroused curiosity—should they wear garter belts along with stockings and reading glasses?

Since I strongly insisted, I finally was able to control one thing freely: assembling the pieces to make a story. No wonder they left me that responsibility. What was needed, was to create a realistic story, apparently. A bunch of horny secretaries was an everyday criteria to start with, with as much suspense as possible, and above all... without any dialogue! Which raises a question—what is an adult movie, technically speaking?

An adult film is generally required to have more or less 15 to 20 minutes of sex per sex scene, with five sex scenes minimum. The final countdown: 85 to 100 minutes of sex, and the movie itself needs to be around 90 to 100 minutes long.

That being said, please do the math of what's left to build a "thriller." Even better, a thriller without dialogue (no, the talent wasn't allowed to wave signs either!). Here, if you lose your Rubik's Cube one day, I recommend you try it at home, it's so much fun.

You may ask yourself, why didn't she coming back to the US now that they were no major projects overseas? I would have, if I could have. But I just had to postpone it a little further in the future. Sometimes work isn't the only reason people move from one place to another, or get stuck in one spot.

A few years ago, right after the *Secretaries* Chinese puzzle, a dramatic event occurred in my family, which urged me to stay in France. Sometimes one has to put things on hold for the sake of those closest to them, and that is what I decided to do.

My niece suddenly became an orphan. Death is always ugly, no matter how you see it. When it comes to someone close to you, it's even uglier. It's like receiving a permanent blow to the stomach, it becomes difficult to breath. It's like some ugly person following you everywhere to remind you happiness is always hanging by a thread.

Remember, when something bad happens in your life, go on and spread the happiness around you. Concentrate all your energy on being happy and going to the next chapter. It doesn't mean that you forget, only that you chose happiness rather than pain.

This decision did not affect my work and I was back on track, as a producer-director, in no time. What came as a surprise were the tremendous changes in the adult industry in a 4-year period. Internet and V.O.D had taken over which pushed many companies, the one that didn't adapt quickly enough, to shut down.

It's another thing with the Internet; products turned out to be way different than before. The level of competition is way higher. Most companies favor quantity over quality. Even if you come up with a nice project, there are already hundreds of them up on the Internet.

And since everything is quite permitted on the Internet, most productions feel obligated to roughen up the sex scenes, pretending people's needs and perversions have increased. It's the "saw it all" with a hint of "we want to see more of it all."

Most of these adult products are made the same way—no production value, just any talent will do. No one cares about make-up and nice outfits, any hotel room will do. It's a constant overbid of anything and everything. So of course the results are very often really bad.

First of all, I believe there is a huge difference between a customer being curious about what's out there (the type that will watch a little bit of everything at times), and customers that only enjoy one particular type of movie. Second of all, I am not against any of it. I just find it shameful to only see that kind of movie almost everywhere I look.

No art direction, no budget, just plain rough sex where girls are often humiliated. Where is the attraction? The fantasy? The eroticism? Is this the image we have of sex?

I don't think so. It might seem too girly but I doubt that watching a close-up of a girl's butt hole for one hour and thirty minutes is everyone's turn on. Especially if she is not enjoying it. Although, wait, we might not even have seen her face, so how could we know that?

I don't believe we are ever tired of seeing beautiful images, with good lightning and nice decor that bring out the best in a beautiful couple. As well as witnessing their sexual intensity as it builds up, which I strongly believe is what makes the scene exciting.

Following my belief, and after 3 years of asking around (fans, friends, people on social networks...), I then took the decision and risk to ignore what the general market reflected and opened a new company with my friend Ron (aka Jon Yuma) so we could go ahead and shoot new lines of movies mainly directed at couples. After all, the adult industry hasn't been doing well recently and maybe one of the reasons is partly because its reputation has been going in the toilet!

I don't pretend to be better than other directors. I only wish to offer a larger variety of choice to the consumers. My goal today is to satisfy the couples watching porn in the intimacy of their homes, meaning men of course, but women as well.

In my opinion, with the exception of a very few companies like Adam & Eve, Penthouse or X Art, production companies make XXX movies for men mainly. They always forget that women are watching too!

One thing I learned from asking all those questions for several years was that women are fed up with "your regular porn." They want more preliminaries and fantasies. They want more cuddling, kissing, less tattoos, nicer looking men, not fucking machine men! They want to see nice clothing and lingerie, romantic locations, perfectly made up female performers, romance sometimes, and a mix of both sweet and languishing sex activities that can also turn to very energetic sex scenes. They don't want gaping holes, spitting, strangling, and gynecological close-ups or humiliated women. Of course there might be some exceptions, but in general, women get aroused gradually.

Evidently, bringing out a girl's assets seems essential, but a man's asset is just as important for a female viewer. Although the aestheticism of the art direction will be appreciated, a small additional touch is necessary for women, since they are much more demanding towards sophisticated details. Bottom line is: none of it takes the sexual intensity away, it's just prepared and filmed differently.

As a matter of fact, it seems like my style in making movies isn't out of date yet or totally absurd. A famous US broadcasting company has just signed an agreement for my new movies, as I finish writing this book, and wants me to shoot a movie per month in that same spirit. They want something different than what they get in the US—exotic locations, and couple oriented. Fits me perfectly!

Shooting the "old way" in Europe isn't an easy thing to do, mainly because the new talents aren't accustomed to it. They show up thinking they'll be done in three hours! I often saw their disappointment or impatience on their faces when I first began to shoot my new line of movies. We had to take special care of them and do some explaining. A few understood the concept and cared for it, as they were happy to be part of a project that will not degrade them.

When I do my pre-production, I spend a lot of time explaining what I'm looking for, what's expected from them. To get rid of the automatism they had acquired for months or years (for example, the exaggerated fake moaning and groaning) is no easy task. Imagine that every morning when you go to work, you get your bus at 9 a.m., then get your coffee at work at 9:30 a.m. and spend the rest of your day say making late macchiato for your customers. Suddenly the bus doesn't come at 9 but shows up at 9:20, so you don't have time for your morning coffee and the espresso machine is broken!

That's a little bit what performers face when I ask them to work for me! Those who understand will do a great job, the others won't be hired.

I still get surprised even after all my time in the adult industry! Never think you "saw it all" because sometimes you realize you are far from it. Like recently in Budapest. A female talent understood perfectly the concept of what I was asking from her, but sincerely couldn't do it. The theme of the scene was a Geisha set up. She spent 90 minutes in make-up, got dressed with a real Japanese kimono, looked at herself in the mirror and cried. First, I thought, "Oh uh, problem with her boyfriend or agent," but it was far from what I expected. She declared that she saw her past life in the mirror when she used to be a Geisha and believed she was possessed by that reincarnation. I guess it's really something you can't control, isn't it?

Imagine the look on my face. Go deal with that! As soon as she removed her make-up and kimono she was all smiley and ready to come back the next day for a "regular" stripper scene (I had to ask her if there were any "stripper" reincarnations in her past lives!). I obviously had to look for another girl to do the Geisha scene.

I am trying to hire real life couples. I mean performers that are either married or girlfriend and boyfriend in their civilian lives but also both perform sex scenes. If I cannot get a real life couple then I have to interview girls on who they prefer to work with and why. It is the same with the male performers. I try then to match them as well as I can. Like on those dating websites!

Back on track, we had to be more careful regarding the heavy shooting schedule for our cameraman, Chouchou (David Caroll). He survived three heart attacks within a few years apart, the latest being ten days before going on our summer camping trip! Lighter days were highly suggested by his doctor.

Completely paranoid about my friend making a 4th attempt on my watch, I remember spreading the word so everyone reminded him to rest when possible, or take his medication on time. Perhaps it made him feel older than he was, but I still suspect he was amazed by how they all did a great job at it! Everybody loves him. It is unfair to see how much someone could be appreciated without even been able to communicate properly, since Chouchou doesn't speak English or any language other than French.

I guess there is something about him. Every Czech actress was all over him, goofing, laughing with him all day long, like he was a teddy bear. I don't know how he does it. If I was a guy, I might even feel irritated by it.

One of them, Julie Silver, once said she would actually marry him if only he wasn't poor. I asked why she thought of him that way, and her answer made me laugh so hard it brought tears to my eyes—Chouchou seemed to have worn the same T-shirt every day and she came to the conclusion that he didn't have money to buy himself enough clothes.

In fact, what happened was that my Strokes-record friend just liked his shirt so much, he bought eight copies of them! I know that it is indeed unusual behavior. Anyway, red as a tomato, Chouchou was overcome by shame and felt necessary to unpack his luggage to show his dirty clothes to everyone. Still, she never married him. Go figure.

Regardless of his shirt collection, David isn't always available for all my projects. Especially when I decide to go away for three obscene weeks of shooting. Uncertain to whom I can really trust in Europe, I felt I had no other choice but to send a distress call to my heavy English accented cameraman from overseas, Barry Wood.

It's quite an honor for me to have him at times, since he still lives in the US, and also because I am aware how well known he is in his profession. I still can't fully understand him, though. It's a bloody shame.

Someone else came along once, when I happened to be missing a crewmember I couldn't replace. His name is Denis. What's so special about him? Everything. He is what I call: evolution.

Denis is the boyfriend of one of my childhood girlfriends. A friend who fell into tears twenty years ago when she discovered I joined the adult industry. She told me of being so devastated that she went to the closest newsstand to verify what she had heard. There, she saw the layout, and cried so much, the newsstand guy himself had to comfort her.

My point being, it takes fantastic open mindedness to be where she and my other friends stand right now. Being able to send her boyfriend to help, without even asking questions or even worrying, considering most women from the civilian's world would have been at least slightly jealous, is a tremendous evolution. I feel so lucky to have gained my friend's trust and I am endlessly proud of them.

Since I had decided to stay in Europe long enough so my niece can go to college and get her diploma, we decided to keep shooting these new lines of movies. We travel all over Europe, Italy, Spain, Czech Republic, Hungary... and try to feature the best scenery and performers we can find. It's a tough job, much tougher than in Los Angeles. Not so many locations and performers in one place.

I have organized my life with a good balance so I can manage both my private life with the responsibilities that go with it, and my business life with all the ups and downs tied to being a producer/director in the adult industry.

Lots of fans ask me why I don't make a MILF come back. Here is the answer to that question. I have given several years of my life to being a performer. I truly enjoyed it and always said that one day I will not do it anymore, and then it would be time to turn that page.

Truthfully, there are too many performers that do not care and would do anything to make a buck. It is not and never has been the way I see things. Furthermore, I think the adult industry is all about being young and wild. As a friend told me recently (as a joke), I'm no Spring chicken anymore!!! I would rather produce and direct my own movies, hire young performers and enjoy directing them.

It's a new chapter even though I have already directed and produced movies for quite a while. I finally have the freedom to make the kind of movies I like without being controlled by a production company. The type of movies I would enjoy to watch with my husband in the sweet intimacy of my home.

I have lots of projects and sure hope I can continue to enjoy what I am doing. The day I will not be able to enjoy it anymore, I won't hesitate to open a new chapter and I will close that book on that period of my life as well.

I have been lucky enough to do only what I enjoy to do and I intend to keep it that way. To extend things when you don't feel like doing them anymore is a huge mistake.

Today, I witness journalists interviewing new actresses and it makes me smile. It's the same old embarrassing questions of 20 years ago. I wish I could warn those girls about the consequences of their choice. But how could they listen? It's human nature not to realize consequences 10 or 30 years from now. It's too far away, and we simply don't care, especially when we are young.

Which is actually a good thing in theory. If we were always to act upon it, we would not accomplish much in life. Evidently I don't want to dissuade them.

Unlike some female performers, once they have retired, I have not regretted a day being who I am and what I've done. Again, the adult industry has its share of good and bad people. No one ever forces you to do something you don't want to do. I've seen too often some girls spitting on the adult industry once they were done with it. This is why the purpose of explaining to a youngster what to expect in the future is important and would prepare them psychologically to be aware that their image will not only be damaged for the time being, but also for life.

If that choice were maturely made when they first got into the adult industry, surely there would be more happy people in our business and probably less suicides or less miserable people.

One day those adult actresses will decide to change jobs, hell, even perhaps settle down with husband and kids (let's be totally crazy!) and that day will require much more strength than she will ever imagine. Strangely, it isn't because we decide to make changes in life, but that life is ready to change with us.

I saw it too many times. If only we were alone in it... but life happens to be full of other people as well (so I heard). No one will spare them. No free "get out of jail" card. It's a tough game, especially when you're young and naive.

Obviously, most people will judge them negatively, and perhaps also the ones closest to them. Even relatives will see them as "different."

Now, thinking that being different can be a plus, outside of Fantasy Land, is rather utopian. In reality, they will always just remain a curiosity, or a freak to some people.

40 years from now, and regardless how many non-sex careers I would have done after the Adult Industry (who knows), I may die at 80 years old from Alzheimer's, and still you will see two lines written on the Internet somewhere: "A porn star has passed away in her retirement home." Then some people will even picture me, with horror, lying down naked.

Being a porn star is very much like being a President. Once you've become one, you will keep that status forever.

In Memory

Duck Dumont
Christian Mann
Leslie Glass
Fred Lincoln
John Dough
Missy
Anna Malle
Henri Pachard
Buck Adams
Frank Vardon
And too many others…

Looking for more? Of *course* you are!

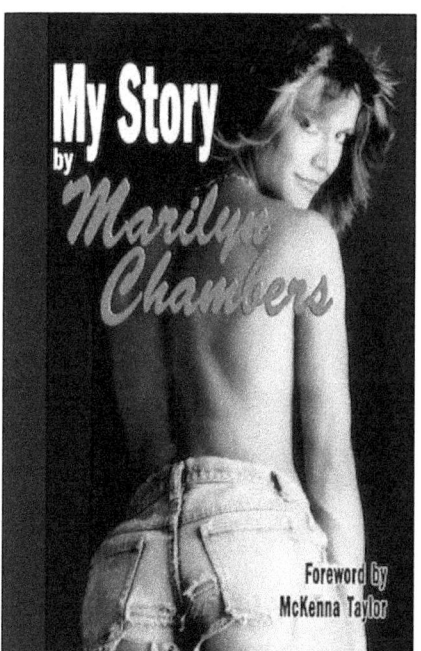
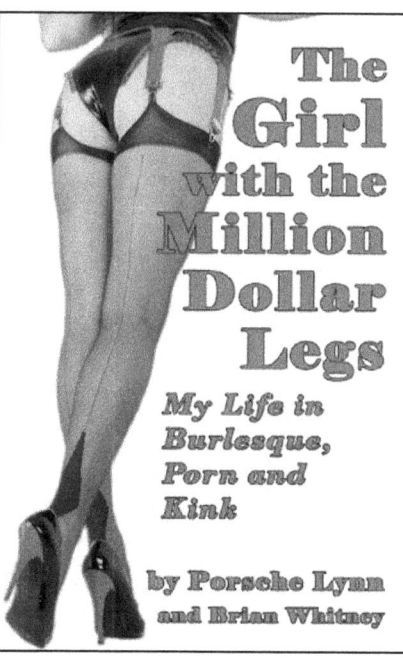

BearManor Media
www.bearmanormedia.com
Hardbacks & E-books also available!

www.ingramcontent.com/pod-product-compliance
Lightning Source LLC
Chambersburg PA
CBHW062004180426
43198CB00036B/2232